VISIONS OF URBAN TRANSFORMATION

Aaron Smith

Urban Loft Publishers | Skyforest, CA

Visions of Urban Transformation

Copyright © 2020 Aaron Smith

All rights reserved. Except for brief quotations in critical publications or reviews, no part of this book may be reproduced in any manner without prior written permission from the publisher. Write: Permissions, Urban Loft Publishers, P.O. Box 6 Skyforest, CA, 92385.

Urban Loft Publishers
P.O. Box 6
Skyforest, CA 92385
www.urbanloftpublishers.com

Senior Editors: Stephen Burris & Kendi Howells Douglas
Copy Editor: Brittnay Parsons
Graphics: Brittnay Parsons
Cover Design: Amber Craft

All Scripture quotations, unless otherwise noted, are taken from The Holy Bible, English Standard Version, copyright © 2001 by Crossway Bibles, a division of Good News Publishers. Used by permission. All rights reserved.
Scripture quotations marked NIV are taken from the HOLY BIBLE, NEW INTERNATIONAL VERSION®. Copyright © 1973, 1978, 1984 by International Bible Society. Used by permission of International Bible Society.

The interviews for this book were conducted by the author and are used by permission. Some names and exact locations have been changed for those who desire to remain anonymous.

ISBN-13: 978-1-949-625-38-7

Made in the U.S

Praise for *Visions of Urban Transformation*

Outstanding reflection on Old Testament promises of restoration in a modern setting. Aaron weaves lived experience with theology as he unpacks God's rebuilding of ancient cities in light of urban renewal in Metro Manila. Aaron's stories and theology grown from living in informal settlements that underwent destruction and renewal are an encouragement for practitioners and those seeking to know more about how God is at work transforming impoverished neighborhoods.

   -Katie Gard: Operations Manager, Oxford Circle CCDA, Philadelphia, PA

Visions of Urban Transformation is a *must have* book for pastors who want to bring community transformation in their respective localities. Dr. Aaron Smith attempts to see social realities through the lens of Old Testament prophecies. He carefully evaluates the systemic problems that urban communities are facing and tries to address these in light of the Scriptures. The most important thing is he brings Old Testament prophecies into life!

   -Mario San Pablo Jr.: Associate Pastor of Graceville Conservative Baptist Church, San Jose Del Monte City, Bulacan, Philippines.

Visions of Urban Transformation will be an encouraging companion for people who have, or are interested in committing themselves to seeking the *shalom* of urban poor communities. Along with relevant and practical examples from diverse contexts from around the world, Aaron's exegesis of the prophetic narrative has a refreshing emphasis on tangible aspects of transformation - food justice, racial reconciliation and communal celebration are but a few examples. Through the stories and reflection questions, you will be empowered to be a catalyst for hopeful imagination for the transformation of your community.

   -Wendy Au Yeung: Site Staff with Servant Partners Canada

Aaron Smith has spent decades journeying with urban under-resourced communities in their pursuit of justice and wholeness. These decades of life and ministry have left Smith deeply convinced that in Jesus the Creator God is always working to restore cities in all their complexity. In this work, Smith delves into the richness of the Prophetic tradition to discover how God has always spoken promises of urban transformation to his people. Smith calls us to hear the words of the prophets anew, receiving inspiration to join in God's vision of transformation in our own time.

   -Andrew Wong: Director of U.S. Mobilization, Los Angeles, CA

Table of Contents

Foreword by Dr. Timoteo D. Gener, PhD 7
Introduction 9

Section I: The Glory of God 13
    Chapter 1: The Sovereignty of God and Transformation 15
    Chapter 2: God's Holiness and Transformation 21
    Chapter 3: God-Inspired Transformation 25
    Chapter 4: Rebuilding to Know the Lord 31
    Chapter 5: Spiritual Renewal and Transformation 37

Section II: The City 45
    Chapter 6: The Downfall and Restoration of a City 47
    Chapter 7: Seasons of Cities 53
    Chapter 8: Not All Development Is Transformational 59
    Chapter 9: Influence and Transformation 65
    Chapter 10: Transforming a City's Reputation 69
    Chapter 11: Love for the City 75
    Chapter 12: Vibrant Community Life 81
    Chapter 13: City Tour of a Transformed City 87
    Chapter 14: A Transformed City 93
    Chapter 15: The Eternal City 99

Section III: Systemic Issues 105
    Chapter 16: Transforming Places of Evil 107
    Chapter 17: Environmental Restoration 111
    Chapter 18: Repopulating an Urban Wasteland 117
    Chapter 19: Economic Justice 123
    Chapter 20: Job Creation 129
    Chapter 21: Food Security for Everyone 135
    Chapter 22: Housing for Everyone 141
    Chapter 23: Restored Health 147

Section IV: Practical Ministry 153
    Chapter 24: Leadership for Rebuilding Ruined Cities 155
    Chapter 25: Incarnational Leadership 159
    Chapter 26: Praying for Transformation 165
    Chapter 27: Repentance and Transformation 171
    Chapter 28: Transformation Starts as a Trickle 177
    Chapter 29: Transformation is Interconnected 183
    Chapter 30: A Reconciled Community Gathering in the Presence of the Lord 189
    Chapter 31: Removing Those Who Are Destructive to the Neighborhood 195
    Chapter 32: Peace and Transformation 201
    Chapter 33: Networking for Transformation 207
    Chapter 34: Working with Secular Governments 213
    Chapter 35: Beauty and Transformation 217
    Chapter 36: Urban Transformation and Missions 223

Section V: Hope 229
    Chapter 37: Dreaming of a Better Future 231
    Chapter 38: Finding Hope in an Urban Wasteland 237
    Chapter 39: Community Celebration 243
    Chapter 40: Encouragement for Rebuilders of Ruined Cities 247
    Chapter 41: What Shall We Do? 253

Acknowledgements 259
Notes 261

Foreword

Doing church and ministry cannot but be concerned and compassionate towards the ubiquitous poor of the land, that is, if the church really carries the name of Jesus and his mission. Otherwise, the church will just become a mere social club tuned in on itself, betraying the outward dimension of Christ's very mission.

Jesus Christ has come to offer "fullness of life" (John 10:10).[1] The apostle John tells us that Christ sends his followers to continue his mission. "As the Father has sent me, even so I am sending you" (John 20:21). Fullness of life happens when God's love in Christ is expressed, enacted, and experienced in the world (cf. John 3:16). Consequently, for Christ's followers of today, there should be no separation between proclaiming Christ *and* fostering social concern or compassion ministries. Both evangelism and social concern go together in continuing the mission of Christ for our time and place.

We see the Gospel of Luke pointing to the same thing. In Luke 4:16-21, Jesus' mission combines proclamation of good news to the poor, as well as healing and freedom for the sick and the oppressed. It is "holistic" – which means combining Gospel proclamation with the Gospel demonstration of healing, reconciliation and compassion.

What you have in your hands is a powerhouse of biblical reflections in support of living out the biblical message or the Gospel of Christ among the urban poor. This gem of a book thus expands the biblical base for Christ's holistic mission drawing especially from the prophetic books of the Bible. Exciting and inspiring true stories of transformed lives punctuate Dr. Aaron's rehearsal and application of the biblical passages and stories related to God's vision of shalom or transformation. What a gift to the wider body of Christ, not just within the Philippines, but throughout the world!

The author, Dr. Aaron Smith, is a seasoned pastor and community development practitioner who also heads the Transformational Urban Leadership training program of Asian Theological Seminary (ATS). For almost twenty years now, Pastor Aaron and his wife Emma responded to God's call to spread the Jesus kind of life in the slums of Metro Manila, but particularly in Botocan, Metro Manila.

I am blessed knowing Pastor Aaron and Emma Smith. Humble, ever-learning, and filled with the spirit of Christ, they model a dialogue of/for life in the slums of Manila for the sake of Christ's offer of fullness of life. Note that it *is* a dialogue, and as such, we are all invited as readers to take part in the conversation; to embody what "Jesus began to do and teach" as his (urban) witnesses through the power of the Spirit (Acts 1:1, 8).

Timoteo D. Gener, PhD
Chancellor and Professor of Theology
Asian Theological Seminary

Introduction

A few years ago I led a Bible study series at a retreat for Servant Partners internship staff that earned me the title, "the Stephen King of Bible studies." I was given the freedom to choose the passages that I felt led to teach on. Unintentionally every passage we studied had either blood or death. Two of the passages mentioned dead babies. By the end of the week, the participants began to joke with me about not being able to lead a Bible study that did not include death.

These comments led me to reflect on my own life. The community I lived in at that time was in the process of being destroyed by the government to make room for a development project. For months I heard the sound of sledgehammers smashing through homes. I often walked through the rubble of demolished houses as I made my way through my rapidly deteriorating neighborhood. Wasted land and ruined communities had been imbedded in my subconscious.

I realized I needed encouragement from Scripture, so I began studying prophetic passages that speak of urban renewal, restoration, and rebuilding. I was amazed at how many rebuilding passages there are and encouraged by the depth and breadth of the biblical vision of urban transformation. These initial reflections became the groundwork for this book.

This book is intended to meet the need for a resource on urban ministry that is hopeful. Those serving in dark and difficult communities need all the encouragement they can get. Scripture's record of the transformation of urban wastelands is a spring of hope that change is possible.

This book is mainly for those already involved in urban ministry, but it can also be useful for anyone desiring to become more involved in ministry in their communities. The prophetic passages reflected upon in this book are meant to put flesh and bone on understanding urban transformation and ways in which we can honor God by faithfully loving our neighbors as ourselves.

This book is divided into five sections: 1. The Glory of God, 2. The City, 3. Systemic Issues, 4. Practical Ministry, and 5. Hope. It is designed to be read one chapter at a time, giving space to reflect on each passage. The passages are briefly interpreted and connected to a specific area of urban ministry. Each chapter ends with questions and activities as a resource to help you apply each passage to your specific context. I pray this will be a useful resource as you continue to walk faithfully with Jesus.

Interpreting Old Testament Prophecy

Before we begin reflecting on the prophetic visions of urban transformation, it is important to examine the basics of interpreting Old Testament prophecy. The Old Testament prophets presented their message either as an encouragement for the people of God to change their beliefs and/or actions or to reveal God's plans for the future. The bulk of their messages are encouragement to change. Predicting the future was not the main role of a prophet. Biblical scholars Gordon Fee and Douglas Stuart write, "To see the prophets as primarily predictors of future events is to miss their primary function, which was to *speak for God* to their own contemporaries."[2] Although many of the prophecies of rebuilding ruined cities are promises for the future, they almost always dealt with the immediate future of the original audience. For modern readers, those prophecies were fulfilled over two thousand years ago.

Prophecy should be interpreted in light of the historical context of the original audience. The historical context sheds light on the specific issue the prophet was addressing. Knowing the historical background is helpful for understanding the intended meaning of the author, and how the original audience would have understood the passage.

It might be tempting to interpret Old Testament prophecy by simply spiritualizing all of the passages related to urban transformation. Rebuilding, restoring, and repairing can all be viewed as descriptions of God's work in the life of the church or believer. While these may be true descriptions of God's work, the visions of urban transformation of Old Testament prophets were not written as symbolism. They speak of real cities being rebuilt. Under the leadership of Nehemiah, Jerusalem was rebuilt. The walls were really there providing actual security for the residents. They were not symbolic of rebuilding the faith of the Israelites.

Spiritualizing urban transformation passages is flawed hermeneutics since it goes beyond the original intent of the author. Another problem with spiritualizing urban transformation passages is that it creates a false dichotomy. God is not simply the God of people's hearts, but their entire body and the rest of creation as well. God reigns over the natural environment that he created, as well as the built environment of cities.

Section I

The Glory of God

Chapter 1

The Sovereignty of God and Transformation: Reflections on Isaiah 45:11-13

Thus says the LORD, the Holy One of Israel, and the one who formed him: "Ask me of things to come; will you command me concerning my children and the work of my hands? I made the earth and created man on it; it was my hands that stretched out the heavens, and I commanded all their host. I have stirred him up in righteousness, and I will make all his ways level; he shall build my city and set my exiles free, not for price or reward," says the LORD of hosts (Isaiah 45:11-13).

Historical Background

Isaiah 40-55 was set in the Babylonian era (612-539 BC). The region's former superpower, Assyria, lost its grip when Nineveh fell to Babylon in 612 BC. This created a scramble for power as the nations previously conquered by Assyria sought freedom. Babylon slowly solidified its power in the region to become the new superpower.

Babylon expanded its control and eventually engulfed the nation of Judah. The leadership in Jerusalem sought to remain independent and resisted Babylonian domination. In response, Babylon captured the city and took the leadership to Babylon. Further rebellion led to a second siege and the total destruction of the city and temple. Babylonian foreign policy regarding conquered nations was to deport the survivors as a way to limit rebellions and diminish nationalism. The fall of Jerusalem meant that the nation was sent into exile.

The city and temple of God were both in ruins. The people were disillusioned and heartbroken. Their world was in chaos. They needed assurance that God still cared about them.

Isaiah's message for God's people was now one of comfort. Isaiah encouraged them with a message that included the repopulation of the city, the building of cities, and the raising up of ruins. The wasteland of Jerusalem will once again clamor with life when the city is rebuilt.

The Sovereignty of God

Isaiah 45:11-13 is within the context of 44:24-45:13 and directly connected to 45:9-10. Isaiah 45:9-10 is a message of judgment to those who were complaining about the way God chose to work. The Persian ruler Cyrus would be the one to rebuild Jerusalem, but God's people questioned that decision. Isaiah presents the greatness of God as a way to grow their faith so that they recognize the fact that it is within God's right to rebuild his city by any means he chooses.

God is sovereign over all of creation. He created the heavens and the earth and therefore he is free to work through whomever he chooses. Cyrus did not know God, but he was still a partner in freeing the exiles and rebuilding Jerusalem. God's sovereignty is seen in Cyrus' obedience. Cyrus was God's agent to rebuild Jerusalem and he didn't even know it.

God is sovereign as he worked to bring about Cyrus' conquest of Babylon. Old Testament scholar John Watts writes, "Jerusalem is the focus of Yahweh's strategy. The call of Cyrus and the fall of Babylon prepare for the restoration of Yahweh's city."[3] God has a big picture plan as he shapes world events to rebuild Jerusalem and the cities of Judah.

Isaiah explained to the exiles that God is in sovereign control of all things. He was in full control when he miraculously saved Jerusalem from the Assyrian siege (see Isa. 36-37). He was also in full control when Babylon destroyed Jerusalem and carried the people into exile. He is in full control by sending his messengers to announce the rebuilding of Jerusalem and the cities of Judah. He is also in control in naming the Persian leader Cyrus as the one who would order the end of the exile and the rebuilding of Jerusalem and the temple.

God is sovereign in our cities today. He is sovereign when a community is in decay and when it is improving. There is no way to know for certain which direction God will lead a community. Regardless of how God works in a neighborhood, we are to remain faithful and trust in his sovereign goodness.

God is sovereign in all situations even when it feels like life is out of control. When a gang leader came to Christ, we thought he was going to be an influential church leader. In the six weeks since he started coming to our church, he showed great potential. He was on fire for Jesus, and attended almost every church activity. He also invited his friends to join. He was highly respected by his peers so when he told them to come to church, they came. Yet, for reasons only God knows, he was killed in a motorcycle accident. Our church was devastated by the sudden death of a young man who had just committed his life to Jesus.

Neighborhood Decay and the Sovereignty of God

Neighborhood decay is a common feature throughout the planet. No place is exempt. Cities, suburbs, and rural communities all have places of decay. Understanding neighborhood decay and the sovereignty of God begins with creation. Everything God created was good. There was peace between God, Adam and Eve, and creation. Creation provided Adam and Eve with everything they needed. There was neither need nor poverty. This was a time when the kingdom of God was in its fullness.

When Adam and Eve sinned, everything changed. The peace between God, Adam and Eve, and creation was broken. The ground became cursed because of sin, making it harder to get food (see Gen. 1-2, 3:17). Creation was subjected to futility because of sin. Creation is in bondage to decay and longs to obtain freedom (see Rom. 8:19-23). Adam and Eve's original sin brought about the curse, but we cannot simply sit back and blame them. Continual sin also affects the land. In Hosea 4:1-4 the land suffered because there was massive bloodshed.

A secondary implication of the cursed earth is the presence of neighborhood decay. Neighborhood decay is a distortion of God's original plan. Before we jump to conclusions and begin victim-blaming, neighborhood decay is in no way an indication of God's judgment for the sins of the residents. Many communities experiencing decay are the victims of others' sins. Someone can have an unshakeable faith in Jesus and at the same time live in a blighted community. Decaying neighborhoods point to broader social sins, particularly injustice and oppression.

Urban Transformation and the Sovereignty of God

Urban transformation is under God's sovereign authority. By urban transformation, I am referring to lasting positive change in a city where the residents, particularly the poor and marginalized, see tangible improvements in their quality of life. It is God's common grace upon a city.

Isaiah reminded the exiles of God's power. God formed them even inside the womb. He made everything in the universe. He is sovereign over all things. Therefore, when God says something is going to take place, there is a confident hope that it will happen. When God "says of Jerusalem, 'She shall be inhabited,' and of the cities of Judah, 'They shall be rebuilt'" (Isa. 44:26) it is going to happen. The repopulation of Jerusalem and the rebuilding of the cities of Judah were as good as done.

God is sovereign over who he uses to transform communities, cities, and nations. God can use political leaders like Cyrus as well as grassroots leaders to bring about transformation. While God does use famous leaders, many people God uses are almost completely unknown. They might not even be our first choice of who we think God should use.

I made the announcement after one service that I was looking for someone to lead our mid-week prayer meeting. I had been eyeing one of the more mature men in our church and was really gearing the invitation towards him. When I personally talked with him, he expressed hesitation. I was hoping that the general announcement would motivate him to volunteer. To my surprise, Amor, age fifteen at the time, said she wanted to lead. I was not thrilled about her offer, but not wanting to dampen her enthusiasm, I subtly tried to get her to back out. I explained all of the responsibilities needed to lead the prayer meeting. She would have to plan what devotional topics would be studied, arrange for volunteers to teach, and if someone backed out at the last minute, she would be responsible for finding a replacement. She was still excited to do it, so I sat down with her to help her plan. She decided she wanted to study through the book of Psalms. She then developed a monthly rotation for devotion teachers and officially took over the leadership of the mid-week prayer meeting.

Since Amor began leading our mid-week prayer meeting, it has been one of the smoothest run ministries in our church. There have been occasions when Amor did not even tell me that the scheduled teacher was not available. On those occasions, she usually took responsibility herself to teach.

Amor has been an agent of transformation in her community. As an adult, she is an elected government official serving in our community. She has also taken an active role in the discipleship of young teenage girls. She has been through the same issues they are facing and has been a positive role model in their lives.

Reflection and Action

1. Where is God's sovereignty seen in your community?
2. Pray for eyes to see God's sovereign work in your community.

Chapter 2

God's Holiness and Transformation: Reflections on Isaiah 52:1-12

> The voice of your watchmen—they lift up their voice; together they sing for joy; for eye to eye they see the return of the LORD to Zion. Break forth together into singing, you waste places of Jerusalem, for the LORD has comforted his people; he has redeemed Jerusalem. The LORD has bared his holy arm before the eyes of all the nations, and all the ends of the earth shall see the salvation of our God (Isaiah 52:8-10).

Isaiah 52 is set at the end of the exile. God has taken away the cup of judgment from his people and has given it to the Babylonians (Isa. 51:22-23). The days of suffering from oppression are over. God is going to act to change their destitute situation to one of hope.

Isaiah begins with the command to wake up. They were to get out of bed. Depressed people have no reason to get up. Rather than face the miseries of the day it is easier to just stay in bed. The city was to wake up because she had urgent matters to attend to. God was coming so they were to be properly dressed and in the right mood for the occasion. After waking up they were to put on strength and beautiful garments.

They were to get up out of the dust, which was a place of mourning. The ash and rubble of the once beautiful city was a constant reminder of God's judgment. They were now living in a new era. The season of mourning has come to an end. The city of Jerusalem would be transformed. Therefore they were to look beautiful and be strong in faith in a holy God.

Holiness in Transformation

The Holiness of God

Isaiah described God as "the Holy One of Israel" 29 times. God's holiness influences all of his other characteristics. Holiness can mean moral purity or distinctness. Every act of God is done in moral purity. God is also completely distinct from the rest of the universe.

The holiness of God is central to transformation. God's holiness keeps the focus on him. Engagement for transformation can lead one down the path of frustration and bitterness. Standing in awe of God's holiness shifts the focus from the city and all its problems to the glory of God.

Isaiah had a deep understanding of God's holiness. In his vision of the Lord he saw seraphim saying, "Holy, holy, holy is the LORD of hosts; the whole earth is full of his glory!" (Isa. 6:3). God is morally pure in his decision to use sinful people to rebuild his city. The imperfections of God's people did not taint God's holiness. God works in and through imperfect people.

Knowing that God in his holiness uses people with all their imperfections is encouraging. It is easy to become overwhelmed to the point of feeling inadequate. At our first summer camp, the situation got out of control when some of the youth stole a kitchen knife and were planning revenge that night. When I was first told that a knife was missing and something was going to go down that night, I was at a loss for how to intervene. I had never thought about what to do when gang members at youth camp steal kitchen knives and plan on stabbing someone. By the grace of God, the excellent team of leaders with me were able to defuse the situation by talking with those involved and getting them to agree not to fight at camp or back in the community.

The Holiness of a Place

While God alone is morally pure, his creation can also be holy. God's people are called to be holy (Lev. 11:44, 1 Pt. 1:13-16). Inanimate objects can also be holy. Some examples include Aaron's garments (Exod. 28:2), anointing oil (Exod. 30:25), and the alter (Exod. 40:10). Places were also called holy. Ezekiel described the temple area in Jerusalem as holy (Ezek. 43:12). The land surrounding the temple where the priests lived was also holy (Ezek. 45:1-8). Isaiah called the whole city of Jerusalem holy (Isa. 52:1).

God has declared that he lives in Jerusalem and it shall be holy (Joel 3:17). The city of Jerusalem will be set apart as holy because it was God's dwelling place. The city is made holy because of God's presence. Jerusalem was set apart and distinguished from other cities. It was the city that for a time was to house the temple of God. While the title, "the holy city," belonged to Jerusalem, all cities serve some purpose. In this way, all cities are in some way distinguished from other cities. Every city therefore has the potential to be holy.

God's holiness is natural and essential. People, places, and things are not naturally holy and only become holy because of God. Righteousness comes down from heaven (Isa. 45:8). God's purification is what makes people, places, and things holy.

The people of God are made holy through faith in Jesus. They are cleansed by his blood, which makes sinful people righteous. God makes things and places holy for his people. The articles in the temple are holy for the benefit of the worshipers. God does not need anything in the temple to be holy. They were made holy to help create a sense of reverence in the way the people came before God. It was to help their faith and obedience. Similarly, God makes places holy for his people. The holy ground was for Moses to remove his sandals and stand in reverence before God at the burning bush (Exod. 3:5).

God can also make neighborhoods holy for the benefit of his people. When we treat a place as holy, we want to see it respected, cleaned, and improved. A holy neighborhood leads the people of God to worship Jesus and love their neighbors as themselves. The transformation of communities begins with the sense that the ground is holy. Therefore, it is worth investing in and working for its restoration.

Reflection and Action

1. In what sense is your community holy?
2. Take your shoes off somewhere in your community as a symbolic gesture of its holiness.

Chapter 3

God-Inspired Transformation: Reflections on Isaiah 49:14-21

But Zion said, "The LORD has forsaken me; my Lord has forgotten me." "Can a woman forget her nursing child, that she should have no compassion on the son of her womb? Even these may forget, yet I will not forget you. Behold, I have engraved you on the palms of my hands; your walls are continually before me. Your builders make haste; your destroyers and those who laid you waste go out from you. Lift up your eyes around and see; they all gather, they come to you. As I live, declares the LORD, you shall put them all on as an ornament; you shall bind them on as a bride does. Surely your waste and your desolate places and your devastated land—surely now you will be too narrow for your inhabitants, and those who swallowed you up will be far away. The children of your bereavement will yet say in your ears: 'The place is too narrow for me; make room for me to dwell in.' Then you will say in your heart: 'Who has borne me these? I was bereaved and barren, exiled and put away, but who has brought up these? Behold, I was left alone; from where have these come?' (Isaiah 49:14-21).

Within the message of the future Messiah, Isaiah recorded a conversation between Zion and the Lord. God declared that his servant would come to redeem his people. Zion responded in unbelief saying, "The LORD has forsaken me; my Lord has forgotten me" (Isa. 49:14). God's immediate reply is the assurance that he has not forgotten Zion, even though the people are in exile and the city is in ruins. God will ensure that the city's future will be a time of rebuilding and repopulating. The land will be restored and the city rebuilt. The city will eventually grow beyond its old borders. When the city is transformed the people will look to God in wonder and amazement.

God-Inspired Transformation

The transformation will be so magnificent that the returned exiles will observe what has taken place and reflect on it. Jerusalem will ask three reflection questions based on the city's transformation. "Then you will say in your heart: 'Who has borne me these? I was bereaved and barren, exiled and put away, but who has brought up these? Behold, I was left alone; from where have these come?'" (Isa. 49:21). The answer, of course, is God.

God is the one behind the transformation. He is the one who will restore the fortunes of the people. The Israelites were powerless to restore themselves, since the nation was completely destroyed. The work must come from God. God took a broken people and empowered them to rebuild their ruined cities.

God gave the people a vision of a future beyond the exile and the destruction of Jerusalem. God was going to take the wasteland of Jerusalem in which the people felt forgotten by God and transform it so much that the residents would be in awe.

Isaiah described the rapid rebuilding of the city. The builders were in a hurry because those who destroyed their city have departed. Having the perspective of being able to look back on historical events, builders making haste is very similar to Nehemiah's experience when the wall of Jerusalem was rebuilt in 52 days (see Neh. 6:15).

I saw builders making haste in Manila in the aftermath of a fire in an informal settlement. Within days of the fire, the residents began rebuilding the foundations of their homes. They were under intense pressure to quickly rebuild because the longer they delayed the more likely the landowner would prevent them from rebuilding. The rainy season was also fast approaching and they would at least need a makeshift roof intact before the rains came.

In a prayer for the afflicted, Psalm 102 is confident that God will have compassion on Jerusalem, and the nations will fear the name of the Lord. "For the LORD builds up Zion; he appears in his glory" (Ps. 102:16). God is the builder of his city for his glory.

Psalm 147 is a post-exilic Psalm that gives praise to God for his work of rebuilding Jerusalem. "The LORD builds up Jerusalem; he gathers the outcasts of Israel" (Ps. 147:2). God is the one who is to receive glory and praise when neighborhoods are restored, rebuilt, and transformed.

In Psalm 69 God is described as the one who will save the city and rebuild cities. The returning exiles would have understood that God's work of rebuilding cities did not mean that God picked up stones and laid them on top of each other to build walls and buildings. The physical labor was done by the returning exiles through the power of God.

The city was so devastated that it was almost deserted. Yet, God was going to change the situation so much that the city would be densely populated. Isaiah revealed that children would complain about being too cramped. For middle-class North Americans, the tendency is to think that low-density neighborhoods are the ideal. However, healthy neighborhoods that enhance quality of life in cities need to be high density.

Inspiring the transformation of cities and communities begins with helping neighborhood residents know that God remembers them. There is the hope that God sees our community, is concerned about its welfare, and acts on its behalf. Hopelessness is feeling forgotten by God. Restored hope comes from a renewed understanding that God is aware of the condition of our neighborhoods. He hears our prayers and acts in love, compassion, and mercy.

The Response to God-Inspired Transformation

The response to God inspiring transformation is to press on with the hard and sometimes discouraging work. Knowing that God has inspired the work of transformation can encourage us not to quit because of burnout. There were several times when I wanted to leave ministry because of burnout. The time I seriously prayed about moving on was right before the demolition of my old neighborhood. I had been in that informal settlement for several years and had worked to help our church plant a house church in another section of the community. The work itself was emotionally draining. One of the young girls my wife worked with to teach her how to read suddenly died from dengue fever. There were a number of murders in the area including an assassination where the killer parked his motorcycle right outside our house. All of those stressors were painful but manageable.

It was the imminent demolition that pushed me to question if God wanted us to transition out of ministry. Everything seemed right for us to leave. We just had our first son, and our community and church were about to be destroyed. We had to move no matter what, so it could have been a good time to pursue something different.

After much time in prayer, we became more and more convinced that God wanted us to remain in ministry and transfer to another community. The decision to stay, in part, was reflecting on Scripture and God's work of rebuilding cities. Our community was slowly being reduced to rubble before our eyes, but we had confidence that God had something great planned.

After spending several months visiting other informal settlements throughout the city, we finally decided to move to Botocan to help with a church plant. It was there that we saw God's hand at work, transforming the lives of the residents and the community as a whole. Our response to God-inspired transformation has been to continue working for the betterment of our community.

Reflection and Action

1. In what ways have you seen God's transforming work in your community?
2. What God-sized transformation is needed in your community?

Chapter 4

Rebuilding to Know the Lord: Reflections on Ezekiel 36:1-38

> For behold, I am for you, and I will turn to you, and you shall be tilled and sown. And I will multiply people on you, the whole house of Israel, all of it. The cities shall be inhabited and the waste places rebuilt. And I will multiply on you man and beast, and they shall multiply and be fruitful. And I will cause you to be inhabited as in your former times, and will do more good to you than ever before. Then you will know that I am the LORD (Ezekiel 36:9-11).

Historical Background

Ezekiel was part of the group of exiles taken to Babylon. His prophetic ministry began five years later. Ezekiel's ministry was to help the people of God understand the exile in terms of God's power and sovereignty. As a people they were devastated and needed help piecing together why God allowed Jerusalem and the temple to be destroyed and his people taken into exile. Ezekiel is clear; the exile was not because of a limitation on God's part, but because of the rebellion of the Israelites. They had turned to worship other gods and oppressed the poor. Even in the midst of Babylonian control, the situation was not hopeless. Ezekiel looks ahead to a time of peace and restoration.

Ezekiel stated God's covenant of peace with the people (Ezek. 34:25-31). This covenant included safety and agricultural surplus. In the restored society God would bring about peace and a strong economy. The social situation was ready for rebuilding the city.

Urban Renewal by God and for God

God will cause the population of the nation to increase and as a result the cities will be repopulated. The depression caused by abandoned cities will be replaced by the excitement of rebuilding. God will put his Spirit in them so that they live in obedience. He will cause the produce of the fields to increase and the destroyed cities to be fortified. Every aspect of the restoration of the nation is the work of God.

Ezekiel makes it clear that God is not working on their behalf because they deserve it. God loves his people, but not because they love him. God's people were not entitled to live in rebuilt cities. They did not earn an increase in produce. This is the essence of grace that we so cherish in the church today. God extended his grace to the returned exiles for the purpose of rebuilding cities.

God will restore the nation for the sake of his holy name (Ezek. 36:22). The surrounding nations profaned God's holiness when they saw the people taken into exile and Jerusalem in ruins. They thought God was not strong enough to save his people. The rebuilding of cities was to serve as a testimony to God's power. When my community in Balic-Balic Manila was being demolished our church's leadership invested in equipping people for ministry. In the years since the demolition the church members have been involved in a number of different churches and ministries.

God is the center of urban renewal. He is the one who does the transforming, and it is for his sake that he is at work rebuilding cities. All of the credit for rebuilding goes to God. It was by him and for him that the nation was restored. We saw God's renewal rise from the ashes of the demolition when we connected with former church members and heard stories of how God has been at work in their lives.

Then You Will Know that I am the LORD

The phrase "Then you will know that I am the LORD" is repeated thirteen times in Ezekiel (7:4, 7:9, 20:38, 24:24, 25:5, 25:7, 29:9, 29:21, 35:9, 35:15, 36:11, 36:38, and 37:14). The phrase only appears two other times in the Bible: Isaiah 49:23 and 49:26. It is mainly used in relation to God's judgment, but in Ezekiel 36 it is connected to rebuilding their city. The rebuilding was not simply so that the people of God would know the Lord. It was for the nations to see the city being rebuilt and know that God is at work.

Life coming back to cities after the exile would point to God. The people were to see and experience the renewal of their city as a display of God's mighty work. Knowing and worshiping God is to flow out of transformed communities. Recently, there was a fire in my community that destroyed about 150 homes. When it had passed, and people began rebuilding, I saw hope in the midst of struggle. The community came together in powerful ways. Neighbors were helping each other remove debris and making sure everyone had something to eat. Our church served as a temporary shelter for those who lost their homes and helped in the rebuilding effort. Several people recommitted their lives to Christ in the aftermath of the fire and at least one person joined our church after seeing how we loved our neighbors in a time of need.

God must be glorified in neighborhood renewal. In the end, it is not about the workers, churches, organizations, communities, or even cities. Everything must come after God. In the context of today's secular society, knowing and glorifying God in the process of transformation is the role of the church. Just as Ezekiel pointed to the rebuilding of cities for the purpose of knowing God, faithful men and women of God need to point to areas in their city where God is working and challenge people to see the work of God and glorify him.

Urban transformation, like all areas of life, needs to be seen from the perspective of the kingdom of God. The gift should not be confused with the giver. Restored cities are the gift and Jesus is the giver. Jesus is to be honored and glorified, not buildings and infrastructure. As pastor Mark Gornik writes, "The future of the city is not to be essentialized, for neither the future nor the city is the center of the biblical story. Rather, the center of the future and the city is the eternal presence of God."4 God needs to be central in the journey of urban transformation.

Rebuilding ruined cities is essentially about glorifying God through loving one's neighbor as oneself. The concrete application of loving our neighbors, particularly the poor, is through engagement for transformation. In the wake of the fire in Botocan, our church's response was immediate and changed as the needs of the community changed. The morning after the fire, several people from our church volunteered to cook and deliver meals to families who lost everything. That lasted about two weeks until enough debris was removed and households were able to cook their own food. After that we shifted to helping in the rebuilding effort by providing construction supplies and distributing donated items as needed.

Isaiah also emphasized knowing the Lord. "Therefore my people shall know my name. Therefore in that day they shall know that it is I who speak; here I am'" (Isa. 52:6). They will know that God is present. This knowledge does not just appear out of the blue. Messengers first teach it.

These messengers are the ones with beautiful feet proclaiming good news (Isa. 52:7). The imagery Isaiah used was based on messengers carrying news of a battle. A victorious battle was good news that brought joyful excitement and the hope of peace. This messenger was proclaiming good news and peace with the announcement that God reigns in Zion.

Paul used Isaiah's imagery to describe the beautiful feet of evangelists who preach the good news of Jesus. Paul wrote:

> How then will they call on him in whom they have not believed?
> And how are they to believe in him of whom they have never heard? And how are they to hear without someone preaching?

And how are they to preach unless they are sent? As it is written, "How beautiful are the feet of those who preach the good news!" (Rom. 10:14-15).

Beautiful feet in God's eyes can be dirty, smelly, and bloody. They are the obedient feet that follow Jesus into the darkest wastelands and proclaim the good news that God reigns. I joined a Bible study in a community near one of the city's dumpsites. The ground was so dusty that my feet turned several shades darker as we visited those who attended the Bible study. The Bible study was held outside and as the pastor taught the lesson, I noticed that his feet were also caked with dirt. This laborer for Christ in a context of dirt and grime had beautiful feet.

Evangelism is proclaiming God's name; it is the announcement that God reigns. The power of the verbal proclamation of Jesus should not be underestimated. Our ministry in the informal settlement of Botocan did not have any successful large-scale development projects. Yet our small groups and other Bible studies were transformational in the lives of those who attended. This transformation was not simply an improvement in moral behavior. Their lives and the lives of their families have noticeably improved.

Joker's life as a teenager can be summed up as being passed out drunk. He was so addicted to alcohol that he could not sleep unless he was drunk. He was someone you would see passed out on the sidewalk and consider totally hopeless. He was someone that parents would use as a negative example: "Don't be an alcoholic like Joker."

Through his friends he began coming to some of our church events. I invited him to meet with me to pray and study the Bible together. Over the next year we journeyed together as God finally helped Joker sleep without being drunk. Joker has been sober for several years now and has taken concrete steps to improve his life. He has now graduated from college and is employed in a respectable job. He is also investing in some of the neighborhood youth by coaching a local sports team. God used his relationship with Joker to transform his life. He went from being hopelessly addicted to alcohol and a detriment to the community to helping make our neighborhood a better place to live.

Joker's nickname fits his personality well: he's fun and inviting, and loves to laugh and make others laugh. It's a joy to have him in our church, and trace what God has done in his life, and the lives of others through him.

Reflection and Action

1. How do improvements in your community point to God?
2. Spend time in worship for the ways God is at work in your community.

Chapter 5

Spiritual Renewal and Transformation: Reflections on Isaiah 58

Is not this the fast that I choose: to loose the bonds of wickedness, to undo the straps of the yoke, to let the oppressed go free, and to break every yoke? Is it not to share your bread with the hungry and bring the homeless poor into your house; when you see the naked, to cover him, and not to hide yourself from your own flesh? Then shall your light break forth like the dawn, and your healing shall spring up speedily; your righteousness shall go before you; the glory of the LORD shall be your rear guard. Then you shall call, and the LORD will answer; you shall cry, and he will say, 'Here I am.' If you take away the yoke from your midst, the pointing of the finger, and speaking wickedness, if you pour yourself out for the hungry and satisfy the desire of the afflicted, then shall your light rise in the darkness and your gloom be as the noonday. And the LORD will guide you continually and satisfy your desire in scorched places and make your bones strong; and you shall be like a watered garden, like a spring of water, whose waters do not fail. And your ancient ruins shall be rebuilt; you shall raise up the foundations of many generations; you shall be called the repairer of the breach, the restorer of streets to dwell in (Isaiah 58:6-12).

Historical Background

The historical situation of Isaiah 56-66 is the post-exilic period (539-332 BC). Cyrus led the Persian Empire to defeat Babylon. He reversed the Assyrian and Babylonian policy of exiling conquered nations. He wanted the people exiled by Babylon to return to their homeland and rebuild their places of worship. He also offered funds for the rebuilding.[5] For the Jews this meant returning to Jerusalem and rebuilding the temple.

The exiles had expectantly waited for the chance to return to their beloved homeland. Upon returning to Jerusalem, they found the city in ruins. It certainly was not the magnificent city of God that their grandparents told them about.

God was faithful to his promise and the exile was over. This did not mean that their problems were over. The returning exiles still faced major challenges. The fulfillment of God's promise of restoration was still in the future.

After a season of struggle has passed there are still challenges. The struggles are still there; they simply come in different forms. The Emancipation Proclamation freed slaves in 1863, but that did not mean that African Americans lived happily ever after since that time. The struggle to confront injustice and oppression continues up to the present. After slavery there were Jim Crow laws enforcing racial segregation. The civil rights movement helped overturn Jim Crow laws on paper, but racial oppression continued. Today the struggle is against the mass incarceration of people of color and the poor as well as a militarized and highly aggressive police force among other injustices.

Isaiah Confronts False Spirituality

Isaiah 58 is a well-known passage on true spirituality, highlighting the spiritual discipline of fasting and explaining true worship as not just showing up to call out to God, but a transformed life that seeks to root out all forms of oppression and exploitation. Isaiah exposed the false spirituality of the Israelites. They thought God would protect them if they followed a few rituals in honor of God. Isaiah knew all too well they were dead wrong. He could not stand by and watch his city remain in ruins because of their false spirituality.

The point of tension centered on how the Israelites fasted. Fasting was associated with mourning and repentance. Israelite law only had one day of fasting each year, the Day of Atonement (Lev. 16:29-31). Weekly fasting began after Jerusalem was destroyed.

Isaiah contrasted their misunderstanding and malpractice of fasting with how they were supposed to fast. The Israelites were seeking God through fasting and humbling themselves. They delighted in God's ways, prayed for justice, and fasted. They thought they were right with God because they were culturally religious. In reality, God was not pleased with their fasting. Ministry leader and community organizer Derek Engdahl writes:

> While the people had all the trappings of religion, it had not led them to reconciled relationships with each other. They prayed and fasted fervently, but did not care about the poor and oppressed around them. It was as if they believed that their relationship with God had nothing to do with how they treated their neighbors.[6]

This is a dangerous position to be in. God was not going to accept their right religious actions because of their wrong relationship with others. Isaiah revealed their guilt of seeking their own pleasure, resorting to violence, and oppressing their workers.

God wanted their spirituality to work for justice for the poor and oppressed. Christian community developer John Perkins writes, "God intended Israel's witness to the world to be a witness of justice. Their defense of the oppressed would make them shine as a light to the nations."[7]

Spiritual Renewal in Chronicles

Chronicles presents the cyclic pattern of rebellion against God, the destruction of cities, repentance, and God's blessing shown through the rebuilding of cities. The transformation of the burned and destroyed cities inherited by the returned exiles was dependent upon spiritual renewal shown through repentance.

Solomon prayed for future generations. He recognized that a time would come when the people would turn from God and suffer the consequences of sin. He also knew that they would eventually return to God. Solomon prayed that God would listen to the prayers of his people when they turn from their sins and pray (see 2 Chron. 6:12-42). The returned exiles would have understood that Solomon's prayer for future generations was a prayer for them. They were the future generation that had suffered the consequences of sin and were now turning toward God.

The emphasis is on keeping God's commandments and listening to his prophets. The Chronicler repeatedly points to God's Word with statements such as, "it is written in the Law of Moses" (2 Chron. 23:18), "according to the Law of Moses" (2 Chron. 30:16), "as it is written in the Law of the LORD" (2 Chron. 31:3), and "as it is written in the Book of Moses" (2 Chron. 35:12). The message to the returned exiles was to obey the Word of God. They were to imitate the obedience of David, not the sinful kings of Israel. They were to remain faithful to God by worshiping him only and caring for the poor.

Spiritual Renewal and the Spiritual Discipline of Engagement

Discipleship that results in transformed cities is one that completes both of the greatest commandments and does not stop with loving God. The second greatest commandment to love your neighbor as yourself is also vitally important. Loving one's neighbor as one's self is a spiritual discipline in the sense that God can use engagement as a way to cultivate our hearts to grow us in Christ.

God uses engagement for transformation as a means of deepening his relationship with his people. The spiritual discipline of engagement works to overcome oppression and at the same time grow our faith in Jesus. One of the many joys of being able to teach pastors and development workers is seeing them grow in their faith, hope, and love for Jesus. I taught a workshop on community transformation to a group of church leaders serving in a destitute community. As a result of that workshop, one of the leaders I spoke with shared that she realized that the Bible teaching in her church was lacking so she desired formal training. She enrolled in a seminary and learned how to interpret the Bible and deliver sermons. Her church's teaching went from folk-theology to solid biblical teaching. The members began to grow in their faith as they learned how to think critically and apply Scripture to their lives. Their church became more active in the issues of their community as their faith in God grew.

The people of God in Isaiah's day were called to return to a right relationship with God. Once they are right with God, which can be seen in their concern for justice, many of God's blessings will follow. Fasting was to be accompanied by right actions toward others. Isaiah addressed the basic physical needs of food, shelter, and clothing. The needs of the poor were to be addressed in their spirituality. Their spiritual disciplines were to be centered on loving their poor neighbors as themselves. The worship that God wanted was one that fed the hungry, sheltered the homeless, and clothed the naked. Pastor and community organizer Robert Linthicum writes, "The most appropriate worship of God is sometimes the service of humanity."[8]

Isaiah ends with the command to keep the Sabbath. The Sabbath is God's protection of workers and even animals, so they are not overworked (see Exod. 20:8-11). Keeping the Sabbath is one of many ways to ensure justice for the poor.

The Israelites needed to live their faith not as religious ritual, but as concrete actions of loving the poor. When the Israelites shared food with the poor, invited the homeless into their homes, covered the naked, and dedicated themselves to addressing the issues of poverty, the city would be transformed. After the issues of injustices were addressed, ancient ruins would be rebuilt, foundations raised up, breaches repaired, and streets restored. Development and infrastructure follow justice. When the poor see the fruit of their labor, a city is transforming.

I visited a former informal settlement that was awarded land rights and immediately noticed the change. Cement and steel replaced wood as the preferred building material. Some of the homes were five stories high and beautifully maintained. Businesses flourished in this neighborhood and I noticed everything from a pharmacy to a pet store. There are several churches in this community. People are receiving Jesus and worshiping him.

Community Transformation and Spiritual Renewal

Isaiah emphasized returning to God in true worship. Spiritual renewal puts Jesus in his rightful position. Jesus is the head of our city, community, church, and lives. Community transformation goes hand-in-hand with spiritual renewal. Development can happen. Infrastructure can improve. A community can look good on the surface level without spiritual renewal. Yet, true transformation rooted in loving one's neighbor for the glory of God needs spiritual renewal. Urban missiologist Sean Benesh writes, "If God's people would turn their hardened hearts back towards him, love and worship him, and forgo their idolatrous ways then in turn he would lead them back to Jerusalem to repair the city."[9]

Central to spiritual renewal was a recommitment to a covenant relationship with God. They were God's people and he was their God. The people of God must submit to the Lordship of Christ and live in obedience to his Word.

The restored covenant was not simply a reinstating of the old covenant, but the creation of a new covenant. In the new covenant God declares, "I will put my law within them, and I will write it on their hearts. And I will be their God, and they shall be my people" (Jer. 31:33). The new covenant was based on forgiveness and a relationship with God.

Transformation is rooted in a spiritual foundation of justice. It seeks to journey with the poor to bring about lasting improvements. It is living as the people of God doing justice, loving kindness, and walking humbly with God (see Mic. 6:8). For this to happen people must be in a relationship with God and living in obedience to his Word.

Botocan Bible Christian Fellowship (BBCF) is a people of God with a desire to live out their faith by loving others as themselves. The volunteer leaders in this church faithfully love their neighbors by journeying with them in the trials of life. The friendships they have with neighbors give them credibility to share about Christ. Evangelism and discipleship are mainly done within the context of small group Bible studies where God's Word is reflected upon week after week. It is through this repeated hearing of the gospel where people come to know Jesus and begin to change their lives in accordance with his Word.

Botocan, the informal settlement in Quezon City, Philippines, where I live has been steadily improving over the years. The community has become much more peaceful, and infrastructure improvements both public and private have made life better for many of the residents. Along with all of these improvements, Botocan has been very open to the gospel. BBCF was planted in the midst of an environment of hopefulness. The church has continued to transform the lives of its members while their community is also being transformed. Faith Gospel Community, another church in Botocan, has also experienced renewal in the last several years and has been through a period of rapid growth.

The majority of the residents do not have to experience spiritual renewal in a transforming community. Even with all of the church growth in Botocan, only a small percentage of the residents actually attend church. Most of the residents do not yet know Jesus, but God is still bringing about spiritual renewal and community transformation.

Reflection and Action

1. What are some common ways that false spirituality is practiced in your city?
2. How can your church integrate spiritual disciplines with loving others?
3. What are you doing to work for spiritual renewal in your life?

Section II

The City

Chapter 6

The Downfall and Restoration of a City: Reflections on Isaiah 1:21-31

How the faithful city has become a whore, she who was full of justice! Righteousness lodged in her, but now murderers. Your silver has become dross, your best wine mixed with water. Your princes are rebels and companions of thieves. Everyone loves a bribe and runs after gifts. They do not bring justice to the fatherless, and the widow's cause does not come to them. Therefore the Lord declares, the LORD of hosts, the Mighty One of Israel: "Ah, I will get relief from my enemies and avenge myself on my foes. I will turn my hand against you and will smelt away your dross as with lye and remove all your alloy. And I will restore your judges as at the first, and your counselors as at the beginning. Afterward you shall be called the city of righteousness, the faithful city." Zion shall be redeemed by justice, and those in her who repent, by righteousness. But rebels and sinners shall be broken together, and those who forsake the LORD shall be consumed. For they shall be ashamed of the oaks that you desired; and you shall blush for the gardens that you have chosen. For you shall be like an oak whose leaf withers, and like a garden without water. And the strong shall become tinder, and his work a spark, and both of them shall burn together, with none to quench them (Isaiah 1:21-31).

Historical Background

Isaiah 1-39 was during the time of the Assyrian empire (745-612 BC). Judah chose a pro-Assyrian policy to gain the upper hand in their struggle against Israel, and to make sure they were on Assyria's good side. They became a vassal state under Assyria so they had to pay an annual tribute and stay politically loyal (see 2 Kings 16:7-8).

Socially, it was a time of expanding inequality. The elite gained great wealth from oppressing the poor. Oppression was rampant and if they did not repent God would use the Assyrian army as his instrument of judgment.

The Downfall and Restoration of an Urban Community

A Community's Downfall

Those serving in difficult contexts are all too familiar with the signs of urban decay. The railroad community in Manila, Philippines, just before it was demolished was a wasted city in which all joy had grown dark. The year before the demolition was one of uncertainty and hopelessness. The government pressured residents to "voluntarily" destroy their homes. The reward was cash or their choice of a lot in a faraway relocation site. The punishment for those who did not volunteer was the threat that they would be demolished regardless so they better cooperate.

For all practical purposes, the community was destroyed before the actual demolition. Urban decay had taken over at an unprecedented rate. Physically, the neighborhood rapidly deteriorated as all home improvement projects stopped, and maintenance was limited to absolute necessity.

A dark hopelessness crept in. Only a year earlier public drug use would not have been tolerated. The persistent demolition threats created a climate where open drug use became the norm. I saw a group of young children sitting outside passing a bag of rubber cement and wondered where their parents were. It was not long before I noticed a group of women sitting about fifty feet from the children also passing a bag of rubber cement.

The downfall of urban communities can have numerous interconnected causes. There are spiritual causes such as the case of Jerusalem during the time of Isaiah. Political and economic decisions can have disastrous consequences for a community. Exactly why a community deteriorates depends on that specific neighborhood.

Isaiah recognized that God was present in the rise of Assyria. He connected the Assyrian threat directly to Israel's turning from God. Isaiah 1:2-23 describes God's displeasure with the sins of Israel, while Isaiah 1:24-31 details God's judgment for purification and eventual redemption.

Isaiah prophesied the downfall and restoration of Jerusalem. He begins with a brief social analysis of the current moral condition, particularly of the leaders. Isaiah ends with a future-oriented judgment, which will transform the city.

The city's downfall is seen in its nicknames. The city was once faithful, but that is no longer the case. Jerusalem went from the home of righteousness to the home of murderers. A faithful city and a city of righteousness describe a city that honors God in the process of transformation.

The once faithful city had become unfaithful. Jerusalem was in the downward spiral of urban decay because of corrupt leadership (Isa. 1:23). The city's leaders were seduced by wealth and power. They are described as thieves who love bribes. Israel had become a kleptocracy, rule by thieves who governed for their personal gain at the expense of the people.

Isaiah confronted greed in his day by warning of God's judgment upon the holy city of Jerusalem. The judgment is described as burning (Isa. 1:7, 31). This is both literal and symbolic. When Jerusalem fell to the

Babylonians the city was destroyed and burned. Nehemiah described Jerusalem's gates as being burned with fire (Neh. 2:13, 17). Burning is also symbolic of refining metal. The destruction of Jerusalem is described as an act of God to cleanse the city of idolatry and injustice.

God commanded his people to "Wash yourselves; make yourselves clean; remove the evil of your deeds from before my eyes; cease to do evil, learn to do good; seek justice, correct oppression; bring justice to the fatherless, plead the widow's cause" (Isa. 1:16-17). This command was not followed. Justice was not being brought to orphans and the cause of widows was of no concern to them. Orphans and widows were the most vulnerable people in ancient societies. Therefore, extra effort needed to go into ensuring their welfare. Israel's leaders were not doing their job of protecting the marginalized.

God was angered by the situation of greed and oppression. Old Testament scholar Joseph Blenkinsopp writes, "The uncompromising tone, the anger and hostility evident throughout, are in reaction to the violence that denies justice to those deprived of power and uses conventional religious practices as a means to legitimate and perpetuate the denial."[10] God acted to correct the current situation. In the furnace of judgment, Jerusalem's leaders would be replaced and the city would be transformed.

Restoration

Thankfully, urban decay does not have to be permanent. Isaiah's message of judgment is not void of hope since restoration will happen. The transformed city will be faithful, and practice justice and righteousness (Isa. 1:26-27). The city's vulnerable population will be protected from predators. The community will be restored when their relationship with God is restored.

Isaiah is not teaching a prosperity gospel. He did not say, "Follow God and you will have a prosperous city, but if not your city will be destroyed." Instead, Isaiah emphasized that both oppression and turning from God have consequences.

Restoration is not returning to the past. At the foundation-laying ceremony for the rebuilding of the temple, Ezra recorded that the older generation publicly mourned because it would not be like the original one Solomon had built (Ezra 3:10-13). Rebuilding is not making the physical buildings and infrastructure exactly how they were in the past. Although some of the more significant buildings may be restored. Rebuilding is about transforming communities to make them more livable and sustainable.

Communities facing the issue of vacancies have to deal with abandoned structures. Some might be demolished, while others restored. A great example of restoring an old structure and reimagining its use is the High Line in New York City. Originally it was built as an elevated train line, but it eventually closed. After years of neglect and under threat of demolition the abandoned tracks were transformed into an elevated public park.[11]

The two main components of Jerusalem's restoration were political and religious. God replaced the corrupt political leaders with ones that truly serve the welfare of the people. This single action resulted in Jerusalem being called, "the city of righteousness, the faithful city" (Isa. 1:26). Leaders who work for justice can change the reputation of a city so it has new positive names.

The oaks and gardens where the worship of fertility gods took place would be replaced by the worship of the one true God. The people were ashamed of their rebellion against God and repented. They will take on the characteristics of righteousness, faithfulness, and justice. These are also the traits of a restored city.

The three-pronged approach in Isaiah's vision of urban transformation was righteousness, faithfulness, and justice. These elements are essential for transformation. Righteousness includes loving one's neighbor as oneself (Matt. 22:39) and looking out for the interests of others (Phil. 2:4). When residents act in love for one another, even a destitute community will slowly improve.

The people of God need to walk faithfully before him. For a city to be faithful, it does not take that many people. Ten people could have saved

Sodom (Gen. 18). One person could have saved Jerusalem during the Babylonian conquest (Ezek. 22:30). Faithfulness is about a relationship with Jesus, not masses of moral people.

A city must be just. Oppression needs to be corrected. Laws that deny the poor their rights or favor the rich need to be opposed and changed. Political leaders are to establish just laws that ensure the welfare of the poor. Government-sponsored programs for the poor should have the goal of helping them overcome poverty and not simply creating a class of constituents that are dependent on the government.

Reflection and Action

1. Reflecting on the history of your community or city, describe a period when it experienced restoration.
2. What were the main components of its restoration?

Chapter 7

Seasons of Cities: Reflections on Jeremiah 50:11-16

Because of the wrath of the LORD she shall not be inhabited but shall be an utter desolation; everyone who passes by Babylon shall be appalled, and hiss because of all her wounds. Set yourselves in array against Babylon all around, all you who bend the bow; shoot at her, spare no arrows, for she has sinned against the LORD. Raise a shout against her all around; she has surrendered; her bulwarks have fallen; her walls are thrown down. For this is the vengeance of the LORD: take vengeance on her; do to her as she has done. Cut off from Babylon the sower, and the one who handles the sickle in time of harvest; because of the sword of the oppressor, every one shall turn to his own people, and every one shall flee to his own land (Jeremiah 50:13-16).

Historical Background

Jeremiah grew up close to Jerusalem as the son of a priest (Jer. 1:1). He began his ministry in the thirteenth year of the reign of King Josiah (Jer. 1:2). Jeremiah continued to minister until after the Babylonian exile. The sociopolitical situation during the time of Jeremiah was dominated by Babylon.

Babylon had established itself as the reigning superpower of the region. Judah resisted Babylonian occupation, but was forced to surrender Jerusalem after a three-month siege in 597 BC. Babylon looted the temple and took the city's leadership into exile. In 586 BC Jerusalem rebelled again which resulted in a second assault on the city. This time the city was left in ruins because the Babylonian army burned the temple and smashed the city to rubble.

Seasons of Cities

Jeremiah 50:11-16 should be read in light of Jeremiah's letter to the exiles in 29:4-23. Both of these are related to the city of Babylon. Jeremiah's letter to the exiles was a call for the exiles to live meaningfully and engage the city for transformation. They were to pray for Babylon and seek its shalom (Jer. 29-4-7).

By the time of Jeremiah 50:11-16, Babylon fell under God's wrath. Their time of conquest had ended. Babylon would begin to unravel and fall apart. Jeremiah stressed that Babylon would reap the punishment for their deeds. The judgment is just. The great city of Babylon would be completely destroyed and deserted. The grand city would lie in ruins.

God in his providence has determined the building, destruction, and rebuilding of cities. Jerusalem was destroyed and rebuilt numerous times in the biblical record and beyond. Jerusalem was burned when the Hebrews settled in the land (Judges 1:8). At that time, they did not occupy Jerusalem. The city was repaired and inhabited again by the Jebusites (Judges 1:21). David eventually moved the capital to Jerusalem, giving it a place of prominence.

During the time of the Babylonian conquest, Jerusalem was completely destroyed and sat as a wasteland for almost 150 years, leaving the city vulnerable to bands of raiders. Under the leadership of Ezra and Nehemiah, the city wall was finally rebuilt. The city was expanded and fortified during the Roman occupation but was destroyed by the Romans in 70 AD.

Jerusalem was rebuilt again and is now one of the oldest continually occupied cities in the world.

All cities go through seasons, but unlike nature, urban seasons are not always progressive stages. Cities do not have to experience every season, nor does it have to be in any particular order. The seasons of cities include the founding, expansion, decay, renewal, destruction, and rebuilding.

All cities experience a founding stage when large numbers of people begin to settle in an area. The founding stage can take centuries where the location was originally a small village that slowly grew to become a city. Other cities are almost literally founded overnight when someone with enough power and resources decides to build and populate a city.

Cities also go through periods of expansion where their population grows. Expanding infrastructure usually follows population growth. During this season construction seems to be nonstop with buildings going up everywhere. The city experiences a boom time.

Cities also go through seasons of decay when the population decreases and homes and businesses are abandoned. New construction almost totally stops as the economy weakens. This season can be temporary or last for decades and completely reshape the city.

Cities can also experience seasons of renewal after a time of decay. Hope is restored and city building happens once again. The city is transformed as life is restored.

Eventually cities experience destruction. Some cities experience immediate destruction through a natural disaster or war. A volcano destroyed the Roman city of Pompeii in an instant. Other cities have been destroyed by war. Cities can also lose their economic base and shrink to obscurity.

A city that has been destroyed can either be permanently abandoned or rebuilt. Some cities such as Jerusalem have been destroyed and rebuilt multiple times over the centuries. However, there are numerous cities that once had significant populations but are now completely abandoned.

It is Not Always Time to Rebuild

The preacher in Ecclesiastes recognized that everything has its time. He wrote, "A time to kill, and a time to heal; a time to break down, and a time to build up" (Eccl. 3:3). For cities, there is a time to break down and a time to build up. It is not always time to rebuild.

Hosea warned the Israelites not to build fortified cities because God would just destroy them. "For Israel has forgotten his Maker and built palaces, and Judah has multiplied fortified cities; so I will send a fire upon his cities, and it shall devour her strongholds" (Hosea 8:14). It was not the right time for them to build because their hearts were not right before God.

Malachi warned Edom not to attempt to rebuild their ruined cities. "If Edom says, 'We are shattered but we will rebuild the ruins,' the LORD of hosts says, 'They may build, but I will tear down.'" (Mal. 1:4). City building against the will of God is futile.

Some cities were to be permanently destroyed by God's decree. When it was proven that an Israelite city completely turned from God to serve other gods, that city was to be permanently destroyed. "You shall gather all its spoil into the midst of its open square and burn the city and all its spoil with fire, as a whole burnt offering to the LORD your God. It shall be a heap forever. It shall not be built again" (Deut. 13:16).

The Cost of Haphazard Rebuilding

Joshua destroyed the city of Jericho and cursed its rebuilding (Joshua 6:26). During the reign of Ahab, "Hiel of Bethel built Jericho. He laid its foundation at the cost of Abiram his firstborn, and set up its gates at the cost of his youngest son Segub, according to the word of the LORD, which he spoke by Joshua the son of Nun" (1 Kings 16:34). The cost of rebuilding the ruined city of Jericho was the death of two of Hiel's sons. Hiel failed to know or acknowledge the power of Joshua's curse.

Curses are not the only concern when it comes to engaging a city for transformation. Projects need to be carefully planned with the various stakeholders. Just because a project is fully funded does not necessarily mean that project should move forward. Having finances and God's will are two very different things.

Haphazard projects can be costly for everyone involved. Failed projects can leave the ones they intended to help feeling even more powerless. One of the haphazard building projects I witnessed was the repaving of the only road that runs on the edge of my community. It is more of an alleyway because it is only wide enough for one car at a time. For all intents and purposes the old road was perfectly fine. It had a few cracks, but it was certainly usable. When the construction crew arrived to dig up the road, I was surprised because I never heard anyone comment on the need to replace the road. I soon learned that it was a project of city hall to replace a road in all of the informal settlements in the city. This was a generic project forced upon the residents of informal settlements. To make the situation even worse, the new road has several defects and is badly cracked in certain places.

Not Every City Should be Rebuilt

There are some cities that should not be rebuilt. This could be because the economic base has shifted so much that the location can no longer provide employment for the population, or the area is no longer safe to live. The nuclear disaster at Chernobyl has made the city of Pripyat uninhabitable because of dangerous radiation levels. Holland Island along the Chesapeake Bay once hosted a small community, but it had to be completely abandoned due to erosion and rising water levels. In these cases, the residents could be helped to move to a safer and more economically stable location.

Called to Faithfulness not Permanent Urban Transformation

The exiles were to faithfully pray for Babylon and seek its shalom regardless of lasting improvements (see Jer. 29:7). The physical transformation of a city or community is about our faithfulness, not its longevity. God may give us the joy of seeing communities transformed, but this is not always the case.

When Balic-Balic Christian Church faced the demolition of their community, the church leaders still remained faithful to their calling of loving God and their neighbors. Church services were held throughout the time of the demolition and continued for a short time after the community was destroyed for those who remained. The church's decision to continue to hold services provided hope to the attendees that even though their world was in chaos their church remained. All of the church-based projects, from a pre-school to soap making, had to stop. Nothing survived the destruction. Although the members have scattered, many of them are faithfully serving in churches in their new communities.

Reflection and Action

1. What season is your city currently experiencing?
2. How can your church most effectively engage your city for transformation in light of its current season?
3. Make an urban seasons timeline of your city and/or community.

Chapter 8

Not All Development Is Transformational: Reflections on Habakkuk 2:12-14

"Woe to him who builds a town with blood and founds a city on iniquity!" (Habakkuk 2:12)

Habakkuk prophesied during the Babylonian era sometime between Josiah's reforms and the destruction of Jerusalem. Habakkuk's prophesy is in the form of questions to God, asking why he is using the Babylonians to punish Israel when the Babylonians were even worse than the Israelites.

The book of Habakkuk is a series of two interactions between the prophet and God, followed by a prayer. Chapter 2 is God's second reply to Habakkuk's complaint. It includes a series of five woe messages against unjust and exploitative actions against others.

Building a City with Blood

Habakkuk 2:12-14 is against Babylon for building cities with blood. The city of Babylon was impressive, but it was paid for with human blood. God heard the cries of those who died in Babylon's war campaigns, which provided the plunder and slaves used to build Babylon.

God eventually judged Babylon and it did not even have the honor of a dramatic end. Over the centuries after the fall of Babylon, the city's importance dwindled until it was completely abandoned until Saddam Hussein built on the ancient site.

Micah also had a strong warning for the leaders in Jerusalem to not build with blood. "Hear this, you heads of the house of Jacob and rulers of the house of Israel, who detest justice and make crooked all that is straight, who build Zion with blood and Jerusalem with iniquity" (Mic. 3:9-10). A city built with violence and injustice stands guilty before God.

God hears the cries of the oppressed that die in the name of development. How transformation happens is just as important as the outcome. The end goal is the glory of God, not impressive buildings. God must be behind a building project. A Psalm of Solomon begins, "Unless the LORD builds the house, those who build it labor in vain. Unless the LORD watches over the city, the watchman stays awake in vain" (Ps. 127:1). Building cities is dependent upon God and must be done justly.

Not All Development is Transformational

Development is not the same as transformation. A low-income community that is demolished and replaced by a highway or high-end condominiums does not constitute transformation even though a specific area of land has changed drastically. There are three ways that development is not transformation. The first is exploitative development related to using oppressed workers. The second is displacing the poor in the name of development. The third is the purpose or result of the development.

The physical appearance of Babylon was surely awe-inspiring. The city was known for its beautiful structures and massive buildings. Visitors would have stood in amazement as they gazed at the city. Yet God saw through the massive infrastructure, which was built with bloodshed.

God is neither impressed nor pleased with urban development that oppresses the poor. The energy and effort going into development projects, no matter how physically impressive, will be a waste of time if it is built by oppressed laborers.

Development can replace poor residents with new wealthier ones. The poor are still poor and, in many cases, worse off because they move to an unfamiliar location where they do not have a social network so vital for their wellbeing. Corporate globalization critic David Korten writes, "Billions face an ever more desperate struggle for survival. By the hundreds of millions they are being displaced from the lands on which they once made a modest living, to make way for dams, agricultural estates, forestry plantations, resorts, golf courses, and myriad other development projects."[12]

Neighborhood renewal that displaces the poor instead of helping them improve their lives is not transformation. Sean Benesh summarizes his experience in the US well when he writes:

> I have read countless stories of urban renewal projects, whether grassroots and small-scale or mega-developments, and they all end up the same ... with gentrification and the resultant displacement of low-income minorities. If that is urban renewal then "no thanks." I'll stick with a corner convenience store selling cigarettes, 40-ouncers, and Twinkies rather than a Whole Foods, Trader Joe's, or New Seasons.[13]

Cities can also be built for sinful purposes. During the reign of Baasha, king of Israel, Ramah was built as a blockade city to starve out the population of Judah by preventing trade since no one was able to leave or enter Judah (2 Chron. 16:1). The whole purpose of the city of Ramah was to force the people of Judah into poverty.

City Building is not Building the Kingdom of God

Building cities is not about building an eternal kingdom on earth. We do not build the kingdom of God. God is the architect and builder (Heb. 11:10).

The tower in the city of Babel was most likely the largest building project up to that point in human history. God did not clap his hands and admire the ability of humans to build such an impressive city and tower. He had to come down to see it and intervened to stop the work (see Gen. 11:1-9).

Pride was the motivator of the project. The whole purpose of the tower was to "make a name for ourselves" (Gen. 11:4). The massive building project was a big ego trip. It was an attempt to be famous. In the end, God scattered the people and the Tower of Babel became a testimony of their rebellion, not of their great skills as city builders.

King Nebuchadnezzar built Babylon with massive infrastructure projects, which both fortified the city and turned it into a work of art. King Nebuchadnezzar reflected on Babylon. "Is not this great Babylon, which I have built by my mighty power as a royal residence and for the glory of my majesty?" (Daniel 4:30). He built the city for his glory.

Massive skyscrapers do not indicate God's blessing. His kingdom is not shown in how high we can build. This is not to say that God does not care about the built environment. God does care about streetlights, clean water, garbage collection, and light rail. A city's infrastructure and massive buildings can glorify God when the people of God praise Jesus for the improvements of their city.

God-Honoring Development

The reason for the warning not to build a city with bloodshed is that "the earth will be filled with the knowledge of the glory of the LORD as the waters cover the sea" (Hab. 2:14). Murder and exploitation are morally wrong and therefore they have no place in city building. Bloodshed and violence do not encourage the knowledge of God. Magnificent cities built with the spoils of war and the blood of the poor are constructed in ignorance of the glory of God.

God-honoring development needs to be done in peace and justice. An example of this from Scripture is the rebuilding of the wall of Jerusalem under Nehemiah's leadership. This development project was God-honoring because it was for the safety of all of the city's residents and respected the rights of the workers. When Nehemiah learned that the wealthy were using the development project to exploit the poor, he confronted the elite and they repented (Neh. 5).

True transformation needs to take into account the displacement of some of the poorest families in a community. Steps need to be taken to ensure that the poorest families are not simply swept aside in the name of development.

The lives of the poor should improve so that they become the new middle class as a community improves. This type of mixed-income community does not displace the poor because the gentry are homegrown.

I have seen many unhelpful and overpriced development projects in my community, but there have been some that have truly been needed and God honoring. One example of this was the installation of solar streetlights throughout my community. This has been particularly helpful in some of the darker walkways. The streetlights make it much easier to walk after dark since we no longer have to wonder what's ahead.

Another God-honoring development project was to install drainage pipes under some of the walkways to prevent flooding. This has the added benefit of limiting the breeding grounds for mosquitoes. It has also made the walkways much smoother. This was a purely secular project done with mixed motives, but the Christian community still praised God for the improvements. Our church did not overdo it. There was no special program or public rally. During one of our regular prayer meetings individual members thanked God for the drainage pipes because they prevent flooding and make it easier to walk. The drainage pipes help improve the lives of the poor and it is right to give God the praise and honor for them.

Reflection and Action

1. What infrastructure projects in your city have displaced the poor?
2. How can your church honor God for development projects that help the poor in your community?
3. Evaluate a current development project in your area to determine its impact on the poorest residents.

Chapter 9

Influence and Transformation: Reflections on Micah 4:1-8

It shall come to pass in the latter days that the mountain of the house of the LORD shall be established as the highest of the mountains, and it shall be lifted up above the hills; and peoples shall flow to it, and many nations shall come, and say: "Come, let us go up to the mountain of the LORD, to the house of the God of Jacob, that he may teach us his ways and that we may walk in his paths." For out of Zion shall go forth the law, and the word of the LORD from Jerusalem. He shall judge between many peoples, and shall decide disputes for strong nations far away; and they shall beat their swords into plowshares, and their spears into pruning hooks; nation shall not lift up sword against nation, neither shall they learn war anymore; but they shall sit every man under his vine and under his fig tree, and no one shall make them afraid, for the mouth of the LORD of hosts has spoken. For all the peoples walk each in the name of

its god, but we will walk in the name of the LORD our
God forever and ever (Micah 4:1-5).

Micah specifically stated that his prophetic ministry was during the days of Jotham, Ahaz, and Hezekiah (742 to 686 BC). During this time both Israel and Judah were experiencing a time of economic expansion. The problem was that the nation's leaders were corrupt. The wealth of the elite was from the sweat and blood of the poor. The more wealth the elite amassed for themselves the more they oppressed and exploited the poor (Mic. 3:1-9). A false righteousness prevailed and prevented them from seeing their own oppression. "Its heads give judgment for a bribe; its priests teach for a price; its prophets practice divination for money; yet they lean on the Lord and say, 'Is not the Lord in the midst of us? No disaster shall come upon us'" (Mic. 3:11).

The economic prosperity of the elite was short lived as Assyria established itself as the region's superpower. Assyria completely destroyed the northern nation of Israel with the fall of Samaria in 722 BC. Jerusalem itself was attacked by Assyria, but God miraculously saved the city from sure destruction (see 2 Kings 19:35-36, 2 Chron. 32:22-23).

A Transforming City Has Increasing Influence

The main issues Micah addressed were idolatry and oppression of the poor. This led to a strong warning of judgment. "Zion shall be plowed as a field; Jerusalem shall become a heap of ruins" (Mic. 3:12). The city will be utterly destroyed. But there is hope. Micah also looks ahead to a time in the future after the judgment is over.

The establishment of the city as the political and religious center cannot happen on heaps of ruins. The city must be rebuilt. The infrastructure needs to be in place before people will flock there.

There was increasing political influence (Mic. 4:3). God will serve as a judge between nations in the mediation of conflict from his residence in Jerusalem. A city led with justice will be one that grows in political influence. Jerusalem experienced a time of increasing political influence when the city was rebuilt under the godly leadership of Nehemiah.

There was increasing religious influence (Mic. 4:2). Micah's vision of urban transformation was centered on the restoration of worship. It is all about God. God is worshiped above all other gods. God's law is taught to the nations. The worship of Jesus as the one true God is what transformed cities are all about. Worship is the end goal of everything we do as followers of Jesus. God is worshiped through Bible study. God is worshiped through disciple-making. God is worshiped through community organizing. God is worshiped through wheelchair accessible sidewalks and drainage that prevents flooding. God is worshiped through rebuilding ruined cities.

Micah's message is almost the same as Isaiah 2:1-4. Micah prophesied, "the mountain of the house of the Lord shall be established as the highest of the mountains" (Mic. 4:1). The mountain on which Jerusalem is located was not going to physically grow to literally become the highest mountain peak on earth. The emphasis here is on religious significance. The nations around Israel worshiped their false gods on mountains, so Micah is essentially saying Yahweh, the God who dwells in Jerusalem, is greater than all the other gods and he will one day be worshiped by the nations.

Micah prophesied that the nations would go to Jerusalem. Jerusalem was the destination of religious pilgrimages, particularly during religious festivals. People were going to the city to encounter God.

Transformation begins with the worship of God, which centers on his Word (Mic. 4:1-5). The spreading of the Word of God and its influence results in the disarmament of nations' militaries. Swords and spears, the military hardware of the time, were made into farming equipment. There will be no more professional soldiers since they will no longer train for war. Nations will no longer have permanent armies that use violence to force their will on others. The knowledge of God's glory will cover all the earth. Violence is finally rejected and replaced by the knowledge of God. The old Jerusalem built with blood (Mic. 3:10) will be replaced by a city of peace.

The increased influence rooted in the work of God brought peace to the land. The poor peasants that used plowshares and pruning hooks could sit in their fields and not be afraid. Increased influence freed poor peasant farmers from the fear of a military invasion as well as the fear of being forced to serve as a soldier in the king's army.

Increased influence must be rooted in moral authority. The destruction of military hardware and using the scrap material to make tools of peace gave them the moral authority to use their increased influence for the glory of God.

The church has an important role to play in urban transformation through faithfully teaching the Word of God. It is true that just because someone receives Jesus does not automatically mean they will be a positive influence in their communities. It takes a passion for Jesus that comes through studying Scripture. The people of God must become a people of the Word. We must study the Bible, be transformed by it, and teach it to the nations.

Reflection and Action

1. In what ways can your community be a positive influence on the surrounding area?

2. How can the influence of your church be used to work for peace in your community?

Chapter 10

Transforming a City's Reputation: Reflections on Isaiah 62:1-12

For Zion's sake I will not keep silent, and for Jerusalem's sake I will not be quiet, until her righteousness goes forth as brightness, and her salvation as a burning torch. The nations shall see your righteousness, and all the kings your glory, and you shall be called by a new name that the mouth of the LORD will give. You shall be a crown of beauty in the hand of the LORD, and a royal diadem in the hand of your God. You shall no more be termed Forsaken, and your land shall no more be termed Desolate, but you shall be called My Delight Is in Her, and your land Married; for the LORD delights in you, and your land shall be married. For as a young man marries a young woman, so shall your sons marry you, and as the bridegroom rejoices over the bride, so shall your God rejoice over you. On your walls, O Jerusalem, I have set watchmen; all the day and all the night they shall never be silent. You who put the LORD in remembrance, take no rest, and give him no rest until he establishes Jerusalem and makes it a praise in the earth (Isaiah 62:1-7).

God revealed his passion for Jerusalem in this passage. He adores Jerusalem as a bridegroom does his bride. God will not rest until he restores the city and transforms it from its state of desolation to being rebuilt. The rebuilding of Jerusalem is a top priority. God will see to it that the city is rebuilt and he is glorified.

God is showering Jerusalem with his blessing and as a result the city is restored and given a new name. The new name reveals its new reputation. The city is now under God's favor.

What's in a Name?

A name brings images to mind. Mountain View and Lakeside bring to mind rustic scenes from nature. One would assume these communities actually have a view of the mountains or are next to a lake. I visited a small and very destitute informal settlement along the bank of a river that was named Sunrise Subdivision. I knew the name before actually seeing the community. The name threw me off so when I walked to the location, I thought I was in the wrong place. The name did not fit the reality of the community that suffered under intense poverty.

Isaiah and his fellow Israelites understood the significance of a name. A name was much more than what a city or a person was called. It was a description of their character. In the incident at the burning bush when Moses asked God his name, he was asking God who he was more than what he was to be called (see Exod. 3:1-4:17). God is I AM. His self-description as I AM is where his Hebrew name Yahweh came from. It is an amazing name. God defines himself as the one who is.

The city of God was called Forsaken and Desolate. Forsaken was usually used in the context of marriage to describe a woman who was abandoned by her husband. Desolate in the marriage context is related to being childless. The names Forsaken and Desolate would have meant that God had abandoned Jerusalem and the city was to be a permanent wasteland. The names were insulting and invoked disdain for the city. The city had been devastated for so long that the feeling of being abandoned by God became its nicknames.

Being nameless was even worse than having a negative name. The erasing of the name of a city or nation was a form of judgment. The Psalmist speaks of God's judgment on the wicked by blotting out their names. "You have rebuked the nations; you have made the wicked perish; you have blotted out their name forever and ever. The enemy came to an end in everlasting ruins; their cities you rooted out; the very memory of them has perished" (Ps. 9:5-6). To blot out their name was to remove the memory of their existence.

In modern times personal names have lost their significance in many cultures. Names generally give no indication of the person's character. However, a community's name may still have some significance. A community's name, particularly its nicknames can say a lot about its reputation. Years ago, I lived and worked in the railroad community of Balic-Balic in Manila. The government's name for the community was simply a number. We were officially named 576 Zone 56. No one actually used that name because a number as a name is essentially useless. We either used Balic-Balic, meaning come back, which is the name of the larger district, or called ourselves taga-riles meaning from the train tracks. The name taga-riles carried lots of baggage with it. For the surrounding middle-class community, taga-riles meant the home of thieves, drug dealers, and thugs.

The section of the train tracks just north of our church was known as Pitong Gatang, which is also the name of an old Filipino action movie. Pitong Gatang had the reputation of an action movie. It was the hub of drug dealing and other criminal activity. Police raids and shootings were common.

The reputation of a community matters because it impacts the lives of the residents. In *Happy City* Journalist Charles Montgomery writes, "Home feels better when it carries a different message about who you are."[14] Living in the exact same house in a community with a good reputation is better emotionally for the residents than one in a community with a bad reputation. It is hard to get excited about your neighborhood when all you hear is, "I bet you can't wait to move out."

Living in a community that has a notorious reputation can negatively affect the residents in concrete ways. James lives in the community of Payatas in Metro Manila. Payatas used to be the city's dumpsite. The perception of the community is of destitute scavengers who find their food in the dumpsite, while the rest of the residents are violent criminals. Taxi drivers generally refuse to drive into the community.

James told me about his experience in a job interview when the interviewer noticed his address. The interviewer automatically shifted to discussing the community's reputation. He remarked, "You live in Payatas! Isn't that the garbage dump where trash-pickers live?" Highly offended, but trying not to show it, James replied, "Payatas is a large community and is much more than just the city's garbage dump." Even though the interviewer had never actually seen Payatas, he knew its negative reputation. James did not get the job. There is no way to prove that James was not hired because he lived in a community with a negative reputation, but based on his experience in the interview it certainly did not help his chances.

An Improved Reputation

A new name sometimes results from an improved reputation. Jerusalem was given the new names My Delight is in Her and A City Not Forsaken. Both of these names directly challenged the old names Forsaken and Desolate. God has not abandoned his city and the new names reflect God's true position regarding Jerusalem.

Other prophets also mentioned Jerusalem being given new names. Jeremiah called the city, "the LORD is our righteousness" (Jer. 33:16). Zechariah wrote, "Jerusalem shall be called the faithful city, and the mountain of the LORD of hosts, the holy mountain" (Zech. 8:3). Jerusalem's nicknames expressed the new condition of the city.

The informal settlement of Botocan is in the process of improving its reputation. Within the first few months of moving to Botocan I was invited to eat dinner with a pastor friend living in a nearby middle-class community. Over dinner he shared that whenever there is property crime in his community the residents automatically blame it on someone living in Botocan. He assured me that he did not believe that everyone in Botocan was a thief. Yet, he felt there was some truth to the property crimes being blamed on people from Botocan.

Over the years I have noticed that some of the surrounding middle-class residents have a less judgmental view of Botocan. There are certainly some who batten down the hatches every evening because they believe that bad people from the slums prowl around at night looking for houses to break into. Others are much more open and respectful. While the standing of Botocan is still not as good as it could be, as the community is improving so is its reputation. The name Botocan itself does not carry negative connotations so in this case a name change is unnecessary. What needs to continually change is the image people have in their minds when they hear the name Botocan. Instead of imagining criminals breaking into homes the name should bring up visions of college students going to class and people working hard to improve their lives.

Reflection and Action

1. What are the nicknames of your city and community?
2. List the names that could be used to describe your community.

Chapter 11

Love for the City: Reflections on Isaiah 66:7-14

"Before she was in labor she gave birth; before her pain came upon her she delivered a son. Who has heard such a thing? Who has seen such things? Shall a land be born in one day? Shall a nation be brought forth in one moment? For as soon as Zion was in labor she brought forth her children. Shall I bring to the point of birth and not cause to bring forth?" says the LORD; "shall I, who cause to bring forth, shut the womb?" says your God. "Rejoice with Jerusalem, and be glad for her, all you who love her; rejoice with her in joy, all you who mourn over her; that you may nurse and be satisfied from her consoling breast; that you may drink deeply with delight from her glorious abundance." For thus says the LORD: "Behold, I will extend peace to her like a river, and the glory of the nations like an overflowing stream; and you shall nurse, you shall be carried upon her hip, and bounced upon her knees. As one whom his mother comforts, so I will comfort you; you shall be comforted in Jerusalem. You shall see, and your heart shall rejoice; your bones shall flourish like the grass; and the hand of the LORD shall be known to his servants, and he shall show his indignation against his enemies (Isaiah 66:7-14).

Isaiah used the metaphor of a mother giving birth to describe the transformation of Jerusalem. The transformation will be so amazing it will be like a painless childbirth. The emphasis is on God's work. He is the one who gives peace like a river, and comfort in Jerusalem.

All You Who Love Your City

Isaiah does not give a command to love the city of Jerusalem. He states a fact by acknowledging that the returned exiles loved their city. The command was to rejoice and be glad for Jerusalem as a result of their love for her.

Love for a city raises an important question. How does one love an inanimate object such as a city? Love is an emotion as well as an action. Love is being glad for the good of a city and experiencing sadness over its pains and problems. Love is engaged in the city through praying for the city and seeking its shalom.

Be Glad for the City

Loving the city is being glad for the positive aspects of your city. The exiles were to be glad for the work that God has done in Jerusalem. Their joy was to be in God because of the transformation that would improve the lives of the city's residents as a whole.

Being glad for our cities today includes joyfulness when the systems work for the good of the people. It is being thankful when there is justice in the city's courts, when infrastructure is improved, and when public space and parks are clean and safe.

Rejoice with Your City

To rejoice with your city is to celebrate with the city. When your city's sports team wins the championship and the city is in celebration it is appropriate to also rejoice. Rejoicing with your city also includes various community events such as arts festivals, fairs, or other events held in your area. It is less about personal interest and more about supporting community events that bring people together for positive interaction.

Community events are a great way to rejoice in the work of God in our neighborhoods. During a visit to North Philadelphia, I was fortunate enough to be there for an annual summer festival. The event was held in the historic Fair Hill Cemetery, which is also used as a park and community garden. This was an amazing neighborhood event designed mainly for families and children. My children loved the pony rides, face painting, and games. Beyond the cemetery fence I could see an abandoned business and vacant lots exposing the painful times the community has recently experienced. Yet, it wasn't the neighborhood's problems that were the focus that day. This was a day of celebrating the great history of their community and the hope they have for its future.

Mourn over Your City

Loving your city by mourning over the pains of a city is empathizing with the pains of your neighbors. It is mourning with those who mourn (see Rom. 12:15). Mourning can help us to more clearly see the pains in the city.

The pains we should mourn over include injustices, wherever they occur. Unjust city policy, which displaces the poor in the name of progress, should be mourned over. Followers of Jesus should mourn over unjust laws that contribute to the hardships of the poor.

Urban decay is something that should also be mourned. Abandoned buildings, graffiti, unusable sidewalks, and litter should sadden us. Anything that hurts communities by adding to the hardships of the residents is a cause for mourning.

Growing in Love for your Neighborhood

It is God-glorifying to love our neighborhoods because God loves our neighborhoods. When we love our neighborhoods we are in a posture to rejoice in the work of God in our communities, and mourn over the ungodly aspects of it.

Many people do not love their neighborhood or their neighbors. Every community has its fair share of people who cannot wait to move out. Some people love to complain no matter where they are. I have even heard negative comments from residents in neighborhoods that seem like great places to live.

As love for a person takes time and effort, so does love for a city and community. One thing that has helped me to love my city has been taking groups on citywide prayer walks. We reflect on Scripture pointing to God's love for the city such as Psalm 46 and 48 as we visit different places in the city. Praying for the city, meditating on God's love for the city, and actually being in the city has helped me to see my city from a new perspective. It was no longer just a noisy, smelly, stressful place of chaos. I grew to see the beauty even with its flaws. It became a place I knew and loved.

When I first moved to Botocan I really did not like the community. My first night was miserable. Our home was not fully finished, and they had just painted that morning. When we moved in the paint smell was still very strong. There was also no doorknob, so we had no way to secure the door without creating a fire hazard for ourselves. It also meant we had no privacy because the kids would peep through the large hole in the door where the doorknob was supposed to be. By God's grace we were able to make our new home livable, but we were still not excited about our new neighborhood.

The process of growing to love my neighborhood was slow. While addressing our housing issues we began meeting neighbors and exploring the area. We discovered some wonderful people and were pleasantly surprised by some of the advantages of our location. A nice park and one of the main restaurant strips in the city are within walking distance from our house. I also spent a lot of time praying for my new community. Every morning I would prayer walk through the neighborhood and whenever possible take the opportunity to talk to neighbors. I met a lot of people this way and God used it to help me love my neighborhood.

Reflection and Action

1. What are you joyful about in your community?
2. What about your community makes you mourn?
3. Talk to a friend about what you love about your community.

Chapter 12

Vibrant Community Life: Reflections on Zechariah 8:1-23

> Thus says the LORD of hosts: Old men and old women shall again sit in the streets of Jerusalem, each with staff in hand because of great age. And the streets of the city shall be full of boys and girls playing in its streets. Thus says the LORD of hosts: If it is marvelous in the sight of the remnant of this people in those days, should it also be marvelous in my sight, declares the LORD of hosts? Thus says the LORD of hosts: Behold, I will save my people from the east country and from the west country, and I will bring them to dwell in the midst of Jerusalem. And they shall be my people, and I will be their God, in faithfulness and in righteousness (Zechariah 8:4-8).

Zechariah spent the first seven chapters presenting the past judgment in which the land was laid waste. The desolation of the land is contrasted with the future blessings of God. Jerusalem will be restored to a place of vibrant community life.

In this passage, Zechariah strung together ten messages under the theme of the restoration of Jerusalem. Each one points to a different aspect of urban transformation resulting in a vibrant community.

Zechariah begins with God's jealousy (Zech. 8:2). He uses the marriage imagery of a husband's jealousy for his unfaithful wife. The message being communicated is that God cares for Jerusalem. God is jealous and he will no longer tolerate a desolate city. God is at work on behalf of his people.

God temporarily departed from Jerusalem but did not permanently divorce the city. The second message explains that God's presence has returned (Zech. 8:3). The impact of God's presence on the city is revealed in its new names, the Faithful City and the Mountain of the Lord of hosts. The city is no longer in shame. God is now in the city, so it will be faithful and holy. It will be set apart by God.

The third message is a picture of the restored city experiencing urban life in its fullest (Zech. 8:4-5). Senior citizens were sitting in the streets and lots of children were playing. The "streets" of ancient Palestinian cities were not streets as we would think of today. "Rather than being conceptualized as continuous pathways, 'streets' were considered outside spaces between houses. Since houses were not ordinarily organized in a regular pattern, the streets were usually a confusing maze of narrow passages."[15] Zechariah described the walkways, alleys, and other open space as being heavily used.

Grandparents and children are mentioned but working age parents are not. Zechariah described the street life in Jerusalem in which the grandparents watched the children play while the parents were working. Old Testament scholar Ralph Smith writes, "In one of the most amazing and challenging statements about measurement of the health of society, Zechariah suggests that we look at the place the old and the young have in that society."[16] Seniors and children are at the center of the vibrant street scene in the restored Jerusalem.

Seniors and children are the most vulnerable in the event of a siege. Jeremiah wrote in Lamentations, "In the dust of the streets lie the young and the old; my young women and my young men have fallen by the sword;

you have killed them in the day of your anger, slaughtering without pity" (Lam. 2:21). The streets were a place of death and destruction when Jerusalem fell to the Babylonians. The city's streets that experienced so much pain and death are now a place of joy and life.

Seniors and children in Zechariah's vision are alive and well. They are doing what they should be doing at their age, sitting and playing while the working age adults earn enough to provide for both the children and seniors. The vision is of surplus, which allows seniors to gather in public places and sit together in leisure. Seniors are not required to work. Likewise, the children are able to enjoy their childhood in play without having to work to supplement their family's income. A broken society is one in which seniors and children have to work.

In Zechariah's fourth message the city's residents see the transformative work of God as marvelous (Zech. 8:6). The level of transformation needed is so daunting it would take a miracle; yet it is not too difficult for God. God calls for faith. The power of God should not be questioned. The people may not be able to restore the city, but God can. The rebuilding of their city is the marvelous work of God. While the people might be impressed with the restored city, it is easy for God.

In the fifth message, God has returned to live in the city that is populated (Zech. 8:7-8). He was not going to dwell in an abandoned wasteland. God will also bring his people to dwell in the city. God intended urban migration so his people will dwell in the city with him. God and his people will be in a covenant relationship. "They shall be my people, and I will be their God" (Zech. 8:8).

In the sixth message (Zech. 8:9-13) Zechariah gives the command to "Let your hands be strong" (Zech. 8:9). The temple will eventually be rebuilt even though it must have seemed like a painfully slow process. The original situation of the city was bleak. The economy had collapsed and injustice was rampant. There may have even been slavery since there were no wages. There was violence and danger. The sense of community had totally broken down. Neighbors became enemies.

Zechariah presents a picture of the past and how bad the situation had become. Times have changed and the city will be rebuilt. God is about to move so join him in the work that he is planning. There is hope. Violence will fade from the land as seeds of peace are sown.

The seventh message explains that God has brought his wrath and judgment, but he will also bring his blessing (Zech. 8:13-17). God's blessing brings responsibility. God commanded the returned exiles to deal honestly and justly with one another. He also stated that he hates devising evil and loving false oaths (Zech. 8:17). Those were to be avoided as the community moves forward to become a just society under God.

The eighth message is a picture of fasting as a description of mourning turning into joy (Zech. 8:18-19). The ninth (Zech. 8:20-22) and tenth (Zech. 8:23) messages focus on the nations migrating to Jerusalem in order to seek God.

Vibrant Community Life and Transformation

Seniors sitting and children playing in the street are a description of vibrant community life. It is worth pointing out that informal settlements are full of seniors sitting in the streets and are overflowing with children running around playing. In this category an informal settlement is a good example of a vibrant community. The pain of poverty is very real and should never be minimized. Yet the beautiful picture of a community where neighbors sit and talk to each other is something that should be preserved in the process of restoration.

Slums are often viewed for their problems, but when it comes to vibrancy, nothing can match an informal settlement in the cool of the evening. My community of Botocan is budding with life. If Zechariah had a vision of Botocan he would have written the exact same words as in 8:4-5. Children run, laugh, and play all sorts of games. Teenagers play basketball, volleyball, and hangout. Shopkeepers sell a large variety of food, clothing, and household goods. Informal settlers have much to teach the world about how to create a vibrant community.

Vibrant community life includes seniors in the social fabric of the neighborhood. A just community is multigenerational. For that to happen both the push and pull factors need to be minimized. Seniors need to be protected from being pushed out by gentrification. They also need reasons not to move. An important feature for seniors is walkability. Seniors need to be able to safely walk to stores and places for leisure.

Vancouver's Chinatown is part of the Downtown Eastside area where there is a high concentration of urban poverty. This cultural enclave was originally established as a result of racist government policies that only allowed Chinese people to live in the few blocks that now form Chinatown. The area is now undergoing rapid gentrification as condominiums and expensive shops are moving in. Low-income, Chinese seniors that have called this neighborhood home are being displaced. Rents are skyrocketing so there is a shortage of affordable housing. Seniors often express the diminishing number of places where they can purchase Chinese groceries and medicines and chat with others in Chinese. In the words of a frustrated Grandma Kong, "Why do we even call it Chinatown anymore? There are so many coffee shops, why don't we call it Coffeetown?"

Various community initiatives have started in Chinatown to help advocate for more affordable housing and services for seniors. After years of hard work, there are some seniors, such as Grandma Kong, who now regularly help organize protests or events advocating for their communities' needs. They are the ones speaking up at city hall to politicians.

In many places, seniors often describe themselves as useless and a burden to society, but now in this instance they are empowered to create change and their dignity is restored. Seniors have opportunities to not only meet other seniors, but also youth and their neighbors from other ethnic backgrounds. Youth have opportunities to grow in their own understanding of Chinese culture and language. They also get to use their time and privileges for causes that hopefully will have long-lasting effects.

Reflection and Action

1. How can you and your church work to make your community more inclusive of children and seniors across ethnic lines?
2. Visit the most vibrant area of your city and reflect on what attracts people there.

Chapter 13

City Tour of a Transformed City: Reflections on Ezekiel 40-48

In the twenty-fifth year of our exile, at the beginning of the year, on the tenth day of the month, in the fourteenth year after the city was struck down, on that very day, the hand of the LORD was upon me, and he brought me to the city. In visions of God he brought me to the land of Israel, and set me down on a very high mountain, on which was a structure like a city to the south. When he brought me there, behold, there was a man whose appearance was like bronze, with a linen cord and a measuring reed in his hand. And he was standing in the gateway. And the man said to me, "Son of man, look with your eyes, and hear with your ears, and set your heart upon all that I shall show you, for you were brought here in order that I might show it to you. Declare all that you see to the house of Israel" (Ezekiel 40:1-4).

Based on the date given by Ezekiel, "the twenty-fifth year of our exile" (Ezek. 40:1), this vision was in the year 573 BC. The exile was not even halfway over when God gave Ezekiel this message of hope. In the year 573 BC Jerusalem was nothing but an urban wasteland. The city was burned, demolished, and experienced years of disrepair.

City Tours and Urban Transformation

Over the years I have had the privilege of experiencing and leading city tours. These experiences are a combination of seeing some of the dominant infrastructure in the city, historical sites, the business district, significant government offices, different neighborhoods, and a sampling of the churches and ministries in the city. Urban theologians Ray Bakke and Jon Sharpe describe city tours as, "A walking tour of a world-class city includes moving around a city and interacting with people and places that make up the city."[17]

One of the more meaningful city tours I experienced was in Kolkata for a class at Bakke Graduate University. We visited historical landmarks such as the Victoria Memorial Hall, and some of the historic churches including Carey Baptist Church, which was planted by William Carey. We visited the Kali Temple and walked next door to see the Missionaries of Charity home founded by Mother Teresa. We also visited an informal settlement as well as several ministries serving the city.

For much of the city tour we walked through the streets experiencing the full life of Kolkata. We observed the old buildings, and passed block after block of vendors lining the streets. We ended our walking tour by eating at a rooftop restaurant that had a great view of the city.

The way to truly experience a city is by walking its streets. City tours should not be done entirely from a car. A car can be used to get a big picture view of the city and for going from one place to another, but driving through an urban area and simply passing landmarks is not a good way to experience the city. This is especially true if traffic is heavy. I tried that before and it just does not work. Most of the city tours I have led are done by using various forms of public transportation and stopping at strategic locations to walk around. The city is experienced through actually being in the different locations of the city.

City tours are one of the best ways to intimately know your city. Physically going to key places in a city allows us to experience that part of the city with all of our senses. We get to see, hear, touch, smell, and in some cases even taste the different sections of the city where on occasion we sample street food unique to that area.

A great way to get a feel for the interconnectedness of a city is by visiting various places of the city and intentionally looking to see how everything is connected. This helps us to see the city in its entirety and get a better feel for how areas impact one another. A city tour can also help give a big picture view of the different aspects of the city.

A city tour can build hope by providing a glimpse of how God is working. I love visiting other churches because it gives me a chance to rejoice in what God is doing. I am hopeful because I know that in the different sections of the city different people are faithfully serving God.

A city tour is different from a prayer walk. Although prayer is certainly a part of city tours, they are designed to be a time for observing, listening, and learning. Thus, they are referred to as a city tour and not a citywide prayer walk. Of course, a city tour can help us to pray strategically. By seeing and experiencing the different aspects of the city and gaining a feel for how God is already at work our prayers can be specific and focused.

Ezekiel's City Tour

Ezekiel reflected on God's judgment upon the enemies of his people (Ezek. 38-39). The defeat of Gog in the land of Magog signified not a specific leader and nation but the general defeat of those who oppose God. The removal of God's enemies paved the way for the vision of the city of God.

Ezekiel is given a city tour of the future city of Jerusalem after the city is restored and the temple rebuilt. The angel took Ezekiel around the city. The impact of the city tour depended on Ezekiel. He needed to go in with a learning posture and his heart ready to be impacted by what he saw.

Ezekiel was to look with his eyes, hear with his ears, and set his heart on what he was going to see (Ezek. 40:4). Ezekiel was to experience the city with his various senses. He was to feel the city. This was more than an academic field trip. Ezekiel was to be emotionally engaged and impacted by the city tour.

The restored temple was the major focus of Ezekiel's city tour. The physical structure of the temple was rebuilt. He observed the restoration of sacrifices to God and the purification of worship. The priests were also redeemed. "They shall teach my people the difference between the holy and the common, and show them how to distinguish between the unclean and the clean" (Ezek. 44:23). This is the exact opposite of what had been the case. Earlier Ezekiel exposed the sins of the priests in Jerusalem. "Her priests have done violence to my law and have profaned my holy things. They have made no distinction between the holy and the common, neither have they taught the difference between the unclean and the clean, and they have disregarded my Sabbaths, so that I am profaned among them" (Ezek. 22:26).

Ezekiel also observed the city's politicians. The princes that govern the city will not be controlled by greed. "The prince shall not take any of the inheritance of the people, thrusting them out of their property. He shall give his sons their inheritance out of his own property, so that none of my people shall be scattered from his property" (Ezek. 46:18). In the city of Ezekiel's vision, the princes will not use their power to steal land from the people. Jerusalem's leaders had previously used their power for their own financial advancement at the cost of the lives of the poor. "Her princes in her midst are like wolves tearing the prey, shedding blood, destroying lives to get dishonest gain" (Ezek. 22:27).

Ezekiel's final vision is of a restored city (Ezek. 48:15-35). The restored city was a place for all the people of God. There are open spaces in the city (Ezek. 48:17). The economy of the city was restored, as the residents were able to work. They were also able to enjoy the fruit of their labor because plans have been made to provide food for the workers of the city (Ezek. 48:18-19).

The Outcome of Ezekiel's City Tour

The dimensions of this city form a square. Ezekiel's vision is theological in its significance. This vision is not the actual plans for how Jerusalem was to be rebuilt. Ezekiel's city tour had deeper purposes than providing building plans. The city tour gave hope and assurance of the return of the glory of God.

The city tour gave Ezekiel a vision of hope for the future. More important than the specific details of how the city was to be rebuilt was the grander image of hope that the city would be rebuilt. Although Jerusalem was currently in ruins and practically abandoned, the city would not remain that way indefinitely.

Simply knowing that Jerusalem will eventually be restored would have encouraged Ezekiel and the exiles. Ezekiel's detailed descriptions probably served similar purposes to a model of a city's long-term development plan. It would have helped the exiles in Babylon to get excited about the possibility of rebuilding their beloved city.

Years earlier Ezekiel saw the glory of the Lord depart from the temple (Ezek. 10:18). The people of Judah had rejected him to serve other gods. They rejected God's law of justice and instead oppressed the poor, so God left. The people of Judah had to deal with the Babylonian army without God's help. The false gods that they worshiped did nothing, and the army of Judah was no match for the military might of Babylon.

Ezekiel's city tour emphasized the return of the glory of the Lord. The name of the city would be "The LORD is there" (Ezek. 48:35). The city was where God dwelled. God's presence would be eternally with his people. Out of the rubble of the ruined city would come a glorious hope. God's city would not be abandoned forever. His presence was among them.

Reflection and Action

1. What might be some of the benefits of joining a city tour in your area?
2. What places should be visited on a city tour in your area?
3. Participate in a city tour in your area.

Chapter 14

A Transformed City: Reflections on Isaiah 65:17-25

For behold, I create new heavens and a new earth, and the former things shall not be remembered or come into mind. But be glad and rejoice forever in that which I create; for behold, I create Jerusalem to be a joy, and her people to be a gladness. I will rejoice in Jerusalem and be glad in my people; no more shall be heard in it the sound of weeping and the cry of distress. No more shall there be in it an infant who lives but a few days, or an old man who does not fill out his days, for the young man shall die a hundred years old, and the sinner a hundred years old shall be accursed. They shall build houses and inhabit them; they shall plant vineyards and eat their fruit. They shall not build and another inhabit; they shall not plant and another eat; for like the days of a tree shall the days of my people be, and my chosen shall long enjoy the work of their hands. They shall not labor in vain or bear children for calamity, for they shall be the offspring of the blessed of the LORD, and their descendants with them. Before they call I will answer; while they are yet speaking I will hear. The wolf and the lamb shall graze together; the lion shall eat straw like the ox, and dust shall be the serpent's food. They shall not hurt or destroy in all my holy mountain," says the LORD (Isaiah 65:17-25).

God is the creator of the new heavens and new earth and therefore he is the center of transformation. The improved lives of the city's residents are because God created Jerusalem for rejoicing and the people for gladness (Isa. 65:18). The people are glad because it is God's will for a city to help its residents improve their lives.

Instead of only focusing on rebuilding the temple, Isaiah emphasized that God had holistic plans for restoration. Isaiah's vision was all-inclusive so that Jerusalem can fulfill its purpose of rejoicing in what God would create.

Isaiah's vision contrasts the city's current condition to what it will become. The city has been destroyed and is a place of pain. There is the sound of weeping and cries of distress. The risk of infant mortality is high. Life is hard and harsh. Even for those who do reach adulthood, few actually die of old age. Oppression and exploitation deprive people of the fruits of their labor. They build homes that others live in, and work in the fields for others to eat.

Peasant farmers today in the Philippines and many other countries face an incredible amount of oppression and exploitation. The whole system is set against them. Land ownership is concentrated in the hands of a few elites. Cash crops for export are prioritized over food for the local population. Farmers are trapped in a cycle of debt just to buy seeds during planting season. In the end, the high-quality food they produce is shipped overseas to higher-paying customers. The farmers end up eating lower-quality food often imported from other countries.

Poverty is inherited, so the children of the poor experience the same hardships as their parents. The lack of opportunities and the power to change their situation creates generational poverty. Those who benefit from the social structure control the laws so that they continue to expand their wealth even if it means that others suffer.

God's laws that were established to protect the poor from exploitation were creatively ignored or revised in ways that watered them down to the point of making them ineffective. The Year of Jubilee (Lev. 25:8-34) would have prevented generational poverty if it were applied. Farmland could not be sold. It was only leased for a maximum of 50 years, at which point it was returned to its original owners. In an agriculture economy, farmland was the family's means of livelihood. A monopoly on land gives the owner control of the whole economy. The Year of Jubilee was not actually followed as it was intended, which allowed the elite to manipulate the economy in their favor at the cost of impoverishing the masses.

Isaiah's Vision for Today

Isaiah's vision of the transformed city is a glimpse of the kingdom of God in its fullness. Isaiah provides us with the end goal of a city founded on justice and righteousness. Isaiah's vision of a transformed city is one in which the living conditions of the residents will greatly improve. It is a big picture view of a city holistically transformed.

Transformation is taking baby steps in the direction of the City of God described by Isaiah. Pastor and community organizer Robert Linthicum writes, "As the people of God, therefore, our responsibility is both to work for the achieving of such a dream while recognizing that it will not be reached in its totality until Christ returns to claim his kingdom."[18] Even if the goals cannot be met, they still provide direction for our work.

Central to Isaiah's vision is a relationship with God. Engagement for transformation must put God first. Jesus must be glorified in all that we do.

Isaiah calls Jerusalem's residents to joy and gladness. Enjoying the city is an important aspect of renewal. The city is not meant to overwhelm its residents with burdens. The joyfulness of the residents needs to be considered. Celebrating holidays, achievements, and other joyful occasions should be a regular part of community life.

Health care is an important aspect of quality of life. Medical facilities need to be available to all of the city's residents. They need to be accessible in terms of location and cost. Social class should not determine one's life expectancy. Health care needs to be holistic.

Housing for all of the city's residents makes it clear that homelessness is unacceptable. Affordable housing needs to be in locations accessible to public transit, jobs, grocery stores, schools, and parks. Those suffering from mental illness need medical treatment and proper housing so they are not forced to live on the street.

There needs to be a just economy. Laws and enforcement need to ensure that the poor are treated justly. Minimum wage needs to be set at a level where it is possible to pay rent, bills, and purchase food. As much as possible employees need the opportunity to work their way up. Someone who starts out as a cashier should be able to eventually become a store manager and even CEO.

The work of transformation is seldom a straightforward process. Isaiah's vision shows the glorious future of God's design for our communities and gives glimpses of the eternal city. What is not seen in Isaiah's big picture vision is that the day-to-day work requires a long painful uphill struggle.

It is easy to read prophetic texts about rebuilding ruined cities without realizing the work involved. Moving towards the prophetic vision of urban transformation requires commitment. Short-term mission trips do not solve long-term problems. We cannot parachute into a community, do a few relief drives and be satisfied.

When my family and I first moved into the community of Botocan, we originally partnered with a church for two years. The plan was to plant a church within two years and transfer somewhere else. We soon learned that we could start a church in two years, but if we wanted to see real transformation in our community and in the lives of our neighbors, we needed a long-term commitment. We met with the church leaders and reworked our agreement in order to allow us to truly journey with our neighbors.

By being committed to a specific location we have seen many improvements over the years. Individuals have gone from being addicts to community leaders because of their relationship with Jesus. The broader community itself has also improved. Flooding is less frequent because of improvements in the drainage. The community has installed a number of fire safety measures that greatly reduces the threat of fire. There has also been a lot of progress in the area of safety. There was a time when criminals were so brazen that they robbed someone at gunpoint in broad daylight. That would never happen today thanks to the fulltime security guards that act as first responders, and the installation of CCTV cameras throughout the neighborhood.

Reflection and Action

1. How does Isaiah's vision of a transformed city shape your goals for transformation in your community?
2. What are you doing to work toward a more just and God-honoring community?

Chapter 15
The Eternal City: Reflections on Revelation 21:1-22:5

"And I saw the holy city, new Jerusalem, coming down out of heaven from God, prepared as a bride adorned for her husband" (Revelation 21:2).

The Bible begins and ends with glimpses of the fullness of the kingdom of God. In the Garden of Eden sin was non-existent and human beings were able to live in an unhindered relationship with God and each other. The eternal destination is the holy city, the New Jerusalem, where there will once again be a sinless existence. The garden is the starting point, but the city is the journey's end.

The concluding chapters of Revelation show the fall of Babylon the Great, the final manifestation of the city as a place of sin, rebellion, and demonic activity. Babylon is described as a prostitute seducing people with wealth and luxurious living. This state is temporary as Satan and the demonic city are condemned to eternal judgment (Rev. 17-18).

Babylon the Great symbolically represents Rome. Rome was the dominant superpower of the time. They used slave labor and violence to concentrate wealth in the hands of the elite while impoverishing everyone else.

The Roman domination would not last forever. The promise is that Babylon the Great will fall. The enemies of God will be defeated. The New Jerusalem will be a place of peace, hope, joy, and love.

In John's vision in Revelation, after removing everyone who opposed God, the New Jerusalem was lowered to earth. The New Jerusalem was made in heaven, wearing bridal clothes. Jesus was to marry the city, which was the community of faith. Jesus wipes away every tear. There will no longer be death, mourning, crying, or pain. Suffering has ceased.

The New Jerusalem is massive in size with immaculate walls. The building materials of precious stones and gold were for beauty not defense. God had already dealt with the enemies of his people so there is no one from whom they need to defend the city. There are no threats, and no one is against them.

In the vision in Revelation, the river of life flows from the throne of God and the tree of life was along its banks. The tree of life produced a different kind of fruit each month, and its leaves healed the nations. John does not reveal the specific affliction of the nations. It could be a specific disease that many people suffer from. It could also be social sicknesses such as racism, poverty, and violence. It could also be the healing of conflict between nations and the cessation of war. The curse will be lifted so the tree of life will provide holistic healing for everything distorted from God's good plan for creation. Oppression, injustice, and sicknesses will all be healed.

The final covenant between God and his people is made. "Behold, the dwelling place of God is with man. He will dwell with them, and they will be his people, and God himself will be with them as their God" (Rev. 21:3 see also Rev. 21:7). The covenant relationship with God emphasizes God's presence and the people's obedience. In the Revelation covenant, God and his people are living together in the city as if they are in a covenant relationship of marriage. God is not way up in the sky distant from his people. He will dwell among his people in an eternal love relationship with them.

The city has no temple since God's presence is everywhere in the city. God himself is the temple. His presence is eternally with his people so there is no reason for a physical symbol of God dwelling among them. The light of the glory of God that replaced the sun and moon is a constant reminder that God is in their midst.

God's Blessings are Now and Not Yet

Is the kingdom of God here now or is it coming sometime in the future? The answer of course is both. Jesus preached that the kingdom of God is at hand (Mark 1:15). He also told a parable "because they supposed that the kingdom of God was to appear immediately" (Luke 19:11). There are aspects of the Kingdom that are now but others are in the future. When we receive Jesus, we enter eternity with God here on earth and in its final fulfillment after Jesus' second coming.

The fullness of God's blessings is not finalized since the fullness of his Kingdom has not yet come. However, there are aspects that can be embraced now. The fullness of life in Christ can be experienced in this lifetime.

John's vision of the New Jerusalem shows a glorious future with Jesus. Revelation was written during a dark time in the history of the church. The Roman persecution was in full swing. The choice given to followers of Jesus was to renounce Christ or die. To choose death was not a pain free humane execution. The Romans perfected the most painful ways to kill people. Anyone who did not renounce Christ was subjecting themselves to excruciating physical pain and death.

The encouragement they needed was to see a glimpse of the future glory. Knowing that the persecution would eventually end provided hope. While future hope is great, it is also important to have hope for the present. Hope is needed to make it through the day-to-day struggles of life. The people of God today need to learn to live in the tension of the now and the not yet, by neither becoming escapist from their community to focus only on eternity, nor losing sight of the eternal city by just pursuing social justice and forgetting evangelism.

If the Final Goal is New Jerusalem, Why Bother Working to Improve Our Present Communities?

John did not write Revelation to give the persecuted church hope only for the afterlife. Revelation is not a doomsday letter. The believers were not to disengage. There are two main reasons why the people of God should work to improve our present communities even if it is not the final goal. The first reason is out of obedience to the commands of God and the second is from an understanding of the present reality of the kingdom of God.

Those who claim allegiance to Christ are committed to obedience. The Bible's commands are summed up in the greatest commandment.

> You shall love the Lord your God with all your heart and with all your soul and with all your mind. This is the great and first commandment. And a second is like it: You shall love your neighbor as yourself. On these two commandments depend all the Law and the Prophets (Matt. 22:37-40).

Obedience is loving God and loving others. Rebuilding ruined cities is an act of loving others when it is done to improve the lives of all of the residents, especially the marginalized. Faith in Jesus goes hand in hand with loving others. Therefore, we cannot separate our walk with God from how we live while on earth. God cares about how we live.

The final destination for the people of faith is the New Jerusalem. While no earthly city, Jerusalem included, will become the New Jerusalem, we can still strive to partially resemble the New Jerusalem. Rebuilding ruined cities is ultimately about moving closer to the vision of the New Jerusalem. God is concerned about the present situation of life on earth. The final vision can never be attained in our earthly cities, but we can work to improve the quality of life for many today, particularly the poor and marginalized.

Reflection and Action

1. How does John's vision of the New Jerusalem provide direction for engaging your city for transformation?

2. List five practical ways you can love your neighbors.

Section III

Systemic Issues

Chapter 16

Transforming Places of Evil: Reflections on Jeremiah 31:31-40

> Behold, the days are coming, declares the LORD, when the city shall be rebuilt for the LORD from the Tower of Hananel to the Corner Gate. And the measuring line shall go out farther, straight to the hill Gareb, and shall then turn to Goah. The whole valley of the dead bodies and the ashes, and all the fields as far as the brook Kidron, to the corner of the Horse Gate toward the east, shall be sacred to the LORD. It shall not be plucked up or overthrown anymore forever (Jeremiah 31:38-40).

Jeremiah encouraged the exiles to be hopeful. God would make a whole new covenant with his people. The new covenant would be written on their hearts, not on stone like the old covenant. The emphasis of the new covenant was on the inner transformation of the people of God. The entire population of the city will know God because of his forgiveness and faithfulness.

God reminded his people of his consistency. "Thus says the LORD, who gives the sun for light by day and the fixed order of the moon and the stars for light by night, who stirs up the sea so that its waves roar—the LORD of hosts is his name" (Jer. 31:35). The sun, moon, stars, and waves are consistent because of God. He is behind them and they point to his faithfulness.

The new covenant was for both the Jerusalem of Jeremiah's day as well as the New Jerusalem to come. Jeremiah's reference to the whole city knowing God and the city not being overthrown, both speak of events finding their fulfillment in the New Jerusalem. The other references to the rebuilding of Jerusalem find their fulfillment much closer to Jeremiah's time.

The Israelites' part of the new covenant was to fear God. The fear of God was for their own good. The fear of God meant they had holy reverence for him. They were not to chase after other gods out of fear of the one true God.

The rebuilding of Jerusalem was connected to the new covenant, signifying the judgment was over. The nation was entering a new season. God has once again returned to his city and the residents would now experience his blessings. The reconstruction of the city was a part of the larger process of nation-building as the people recommitted themselves to God.

The rebuilding of Jerusalem is not simply a replacement of the old. The city will not be rebuilt as a replica of how it used to be. The new city will be bigger and better. The measuring line shall go out further. It will not stop at the old boundaries of the city.

In the New Testament, the letter to the Hebrews quotes from Jeremiah 31:31-34. Jesus is the high priest and mediator of a new covenant. Jesus did not simply restore the old covenant; he brought about a new and better covenant.

Rebuilding decaying neighborhoods is for the Lord. It is for his glory because it is a visible sign of his faithfulness. Being rebuilt for God undercuts selfishness and pride. Kings, governors, and officials would not be honored for the city's improvements. God and God alone would receive all the glory and honor for the work of rebuilding his city.

Transforming Places of Evil to be Holy

There are places of sin in the brokenness of today's cities. Yet, none of it is too far gone for God to redeem. The previous owner of the building where our church meets ran an illegal gambling den and worked as a fortune-teller before she died. The same place where people once came to win easy money or to invoke the spirits to favor them is now where Jesus is worshiped. The same physical location that once offered false hope is now where people find true hope in Jesus. The change happened when the owner's son inherited the property. He dedicated it to God and wanted to use it as a place of worship. For years he gave our church free use of the first floor of the building. When he sold the property, part of the sales agreement was that the church was to continue to have rent-free use of the first floor indefinitely. God is glorified through his transforming a former place of sin to a place where Jesus is worshiped.

The rebuilding of Jerusalem was on unholy ground. It was the location of unimaginable sins. The valley of the dead bodies was a place of child sacrifice (Jer. 7:31). Jeremiah's use of the term *ashes* (Jer. 31:40) is most likely a reference to human sacrifices. This valley was a place of great suffering. Blood has polluted the land. It was a place of evil.

In the Jewish understanding, uncleanness spread by contact. Dead bodies were unclean so if anyone came into contact with a dead body, they were made unclean. A place filled with the ashes of human sacrifices to false gods was so unclean that any respectable Jew would not go anywhere near it. It was a place to be avoided.

God did the impossible. He purified a place that was formerly cast off as unredeemable. God's plan was not to annihilate the place of sin but to transform it. God took the place made unclean by people burning their children to death and made it holy ground. The unclean urban outskirts will be sacred to the Lord. His holiness is more powerful than unclean defilement. God purposefully extends into places that were once thought unredeemable.

Prayer Walking

Transforming places of evil enters the area of spiritual warfare. Author and leader John Dawson writes, "Christians are called to operate in the unseen realm. We must take initiative to take territory from Satan."[19] This is an important role of intercessory prayer. Prayers for oppressed communities seek justice in places of injustice. God uses prayer to transform communities. Prayer and specifically prayer walking is an important part of transforming places of evil. By being out in the neighborhood, prayer walking helps to inform prayers making them more specific and strategic. Prayer for a community while being in it allows our prayers to be shaped by the current situation of the neighborhood at that specific time. We are able to pray for total strangers we pass on the street. Prayer walking is a great way to grow in sensitivity to the movement of the Spirit by being attentive to what we are seeing, hearing, experiencing, and even smelling. It allows us to be open to the Holy Spirit's guidance to inform our prayers.

Prayer walking is a vital part of engaging your community for transformation. Our church encourages its members to prayer walk in our neighborhood in order to pray for the community. The feedback has been positive, as they grow more passionate about asking God to transform their community.

When we first moved into Botocan the only thing we did for the first several months was prayer walk and talk with local residents. One of my early prayers for the community was for God to make my neighborhood a place of worship. God has answered that prayer not only for our church, but also for the other churches in Botocan across denominational lines. Much of the early fruit that we saw in our work is attributed to the movement of God's Spirit through those initial prayer walks.

Reflection and Action

1. What areas in your city are considered places of sin?
2. What might transformation look like in those places?
3. Prayer walk in your community.

Chapter 17

Environmental Restoration: Reflections on Isaiah 35:1-10

Say to those who have an anxious heart, "Be strong; fear not! Behold, your God will come with vengeance, with the recompense of God. He will come and save you." Then the eyes of the blind shall be opened, and the ears of the deaf unstopped; then shall the lame man leap like a deer, and the tongue of the mute sing for joy. For waters break forth in the wilderness, and streams in the desert; the burning sand shall become a pool, and the thirsty ground springs of water; in the haunt of jackals, where they lie down, the grass shall become reeds and rushes. And a highway shall be there, and it shall be called the Way of Holiness; the unclean shall not pass over it. It shall belong to those who walk on the way; even if they are fools, they shall not go astray. No lion shall be there, nor shall any ravenous beast come up on it; they shall not be found there, but the redeemed shall walk there. And the ransomed of the LORD shall return and come to Zion with singing; everlasting joy shall be upon their heads; they shall obtain gladness and joy, and sorrow and sighing shall flee away (Isaiah 35:4-10).

Sandwiched between prophesies on the destruction of the cities of Edom and a description of the Assyrian siege of Jerusalem is a message of hope. Isaiah 35 is a vision of Jerusalem restored. The image is of joy, restored strength, physical healing, and a highway leading to Jerusalem.

The returning exiles will travel on the highway to Jerusalem. The highway would be called the Way of Holiness. The dirt and stones that make up the road were made holy because the people returning to rebuild Jerusalem would use the road. The way of holiness is a description of the redeemed exiles who walked to the city after the time of judgment was over. They have faced judgment, and in the process, have been purified. There is a renewed commitment to live in obedience to God's commands.

The transformed city of Isaiah 35 stands in contrast to the destruction of Edom in Isaiah 34. The wild animals that are in the ruined city of Edom (Isa. 34:11-15) cannot be found in Jerusalem. The city will not remain a deserted wasteland. People are moving back in so wild animals that fear people will not be around. The absence of dangerous animals emphasizes that they are in a time of peace. The judgment is over, and the time of redemption has begun.

Water heals the parched land. Rains can turn a dry desert into a lush meadow teeming with life. The ecology is restored. Biblical scholar Christopher Wright writes, "There is an ecological dimension to the full biblical understanding of God's saving purpose which should not be overlooked."[20] God cares about the land and acts to transform a dry wilderness into a place that can sustain life.

The transformation of the wasteland was an emotional event. The people were filled with joy and gladness as they shouted with excitement. They saw the land green with life, and they were overjoyed.

A Transformed City Has a Positive Impact on the Countryside

Too often cities negatively impact the land around them. The ecological footprint of urban pollution spreads to neighboring areas. If you walk along the banks of many of Manila's waterways, you may see children rafting through a sea of floating trash. The current is fairly stagnant, so these islands of garbage not only stink up the neighborhood, but also find their way into the neighborhoods downstream and outside the city.[21] Urban problems can also show up far from the city where they originated. Street gangs that originally started in the city are finding their way into rural communities, and even spreading internationally.

Cities can positively impact the area around them. Ezekiel had a vision of a river flowing from the temple in Jerusalem that brought life to the ravaged land (Ezek. 47:1-12). In his vision, the river made even the Dead Sea come to life with an abundance of fish providing sustenance to the local population.

The river is able to sustain a wide variety of trees growing on both sides of the banks. The trees are miraculously productive. The fruit of the trees provides a constant source of food, and the leaves are for healing. The river provides the life support for the entire population. The land experiences God's miraculous healing. It is made even better than it was before the exile.

The transformed city has a positive environmental effect on the surrounding countryside. Instead of dumping pollutants into the air, land, and water, a city can take steps to curb its ecological footprint and to influence rural areas to follow suit.

Urban Transformation and Restoring the Natural Environment

The residents of South Los Angeles fighting against energy companies drilling for oil in their community is one example of working for the restoration of the natural environment. In my own neighborhood, it is as simple as rooftop gardens, composting, and trying to recycle and reuse as much as possible to limit actual waste.

Restoring the natural environment in the city includes both the creation of healthy green space and limiting the ecological footprint. Healthy green spaces can include tree planting, river restoration, urban gardening, and a host of other creative ways to help with environmental restoration.

Healthy green space does not necessarily have to be green. Cities in dry environments such as Los Angeles should make use of native plants that do not need fertilizer or extra water, not lush green grass imported from wetter ecosystems.

Large manicured lawns should not be misjudged as being environmentally friendly because of the need for water, chemical fertilizers, herbicides, and mowing. Some churches have dug up their lawns and replaced them with community gardens. Community gardens might not always look as nice as lawns, but they can be a better use of land. They allow the residents to reconnect with the natural environment, encourage composting, and provide fresh healthy food.

Restoring the natural environment is both a policy issue for governments and personal lifestyle choices. Both need to be in place as we work for the transformation of our cities. There are numerous ways to be engaged for environmental restoration. Reduce, reuse, and recycle are common ways to approach environmentalism. Of the three, reduce is probably the most important but also the most ignored. Reducing goes against the culture of consumerism.

The way for cities to sustainably reduce is through neighborhood design. The neighborhood design of combining commercial and residential sectors into mixed-use, mixed-income communities that are walkable can reduce a city's impact on the surrounding countryside. This is the only way to stop sprawl from destroying rural communities and the environment.

Mixed-use, mixed-income communities are essential for environmentally friendly cities. Commercial activity that can be done simply by walking greatly reduces the number of miles driven. Local owners limit the number of people that have to commute to work.

Urban car ownership needs to be optional. Walking and biking are environmentally friendly ways to travel. It helps the environment by eliminating harmful emissions from cars, which reduces the amount of greenhouse gases that are released into the atmosphere. The improved air quality in and of itself is a huge benefit to the environment.

Restoring the natural environment is a justice issue because the poor are the ones that suffer the most from environmental destruction. The poor also suffer in the name of environmentalism. Environmentalism is a common excuse for the government to destroy the homes of the poor and force them to move. This is not a justifiable reason to cause the suffering of the poor. Informal settlements and tent cities are often tucked away near waterways. The lack of city services such as sewage or trash removal results in a lot of garbage and human waste piling up. The blame for pollution is put on the poor instead of on the city's refusal to provide basic services. Forcing the poor to move because of their impact on the environment fails to hold the city accountable for their oppression of the poor. Environmental restoration is not justifiable when it displaces the poor.

Reflection and Action

1. What are the environmental issues in your area that need to be addressed?
2. What concrete steps can you take to limit the number of times per week that you drive, and the distance you travel per trip?

Chapter 18

Repopulating an Urban Wasteland: Reflections on Jeremiah 30:17-22

For I will restore health to you, and your wounds I will heal, declares the LORD, because they have called you an outcast: 'It is Zion, for whom no one cares!' Thus says the LORD: Behold, I will restore the fortunes of the tents of Jacob and have compassion on his dwellings; the city shall be rebuilt on its mound, and the palace shall stand where it used to be. Out of them shall come songs of thanksgiving, and the voices of those who celebrate. I will multiply them, and they shall not be few; I will make them honored, and they shall not be small. Their children shall be as they were of old, and their congregation shall be established before me, and I will punish all who oppress them. Their prince shall be one of themselves; their ruler shall come out from their midst; I will make him draw near, and he shall approach me, for who would dare of himself to approach me? declares the LORD. And you shall be my people and I will be your God (Jeremiah 30:17-22).

The defeat of Jerusalem at the hands of Babylon and the subsequent exile was devastating. The people needed to know that the loss of Jerusalem was not because the Babylonian gods were stronger than the one true God, but because of their unfaithfulness. They also needed to know that Babylon's capture of Jerusalem was not the end of the story. There was hope of restoration. The exile would eventually end, and Jerusalem would be rebuilt.

Jeremiah 30-33 focuses on the restoration of the nation and their covenant with God. Within this larger section are several distinct visions of urban transformation. God will heal their wounds, restore their health, and not allow others to insult his city by calling her an outcast (Jer. 30:12-17). God cares for his city and acts on her behalf. In compassion, the heap of ruins of the destroyed city will be rebuilt.

Jeremiah envisioned the complete restoration of the ruined city. They will have restored health (Jer. 30:17), restored fortunes (Jer. 30:18), celebration and thanksgiving, population growth, growing in significance (Jer. 30:19), God's protection from oppressors (Jer. 30:20), local leadership, and a recommitment as the people of God (Jer. 30:22).

Repopulation and Urban Transformation

God will multiply the city's population (Jer. 30:19). The city that was once uninhabited is now being repopulated by an act of God. The strategy for repopulation was the intentional relocation to the urban wastelands of Jerusalem and the other destroyed cities in Judah.

Other prophets pick up the theme of repopulating an urban wasteland. Zechariah saw the city's population increase so much that they would not fit within the city's walls (Zech. 2:4). Isaiah noted that God did not create the earth to be empty; he made it to be inhabited (Isa. 45:18). Cities were meant to be bustling with life.

Vacant lots and deserted homes and businesses are not God's design for cities. Abandoned buildings can result in an increase in criminal activity and the worsening of a neighborhood. Repopulating a community limits the number of vacant buildings, helping to improve the area.

God will ensure that the desolate city would increase in population so much that it would become crowded. The current trend is to have a negative view of urban density. During the time of the prophets, a vacant and unpopulated city was one under judgment, while a populated one was blessed by God. Watts writes, "The city's growth is cited as an unmistakable sign of Yahweh's grace."[22] The high population density portrayed in this passage shows the abundant blessing of God.

'Repopulated' and 'overcrowded' should not be confused. Low-income neighborhoods are often associated with overcrowding and the related health and social problems. Overcrowding is an issue for specific households and not communities as a whole. Overcrowding and depopulation can happen simultaneously. Families can be evicted, and their houses remain vacant since the owner thinks they can eventually earn more by simply sitting on the property as opposed to renting it at a lower rate. When this happens, some people will move away reducing the total population of the area. But others will jointly rent in the same area causing that specific home to be overcrowded.

Healthy population density is vital for communities. There needs to be enough people in a community to make local businesses and government services sustainable. A healthy population density means a solid tax base to fund government programs and for businesses to have enough of a customer base to be profitable.

While some people may cherish zero population growth, these areas are not as romantic as our imagination might make them out to be. Zero population growth can be a sign of an area that is struggling economically.

Urban transformation in communities plagued by vacant homes and abandoned businesses caused by depopulation requires intentional work to repopulate the community. A few committed families and singles relocating to a depopulated community can be the initial steps in revitalizing a neighborhood. I am greatly encouraged by the number of young adults fresh out of college who are moving into places of urban decay for the purpose of engaging their community for transformation.

Those with resources that move into blighted urban neighborhoods must be committed to serving their community for the good of the original residents and not simply for higher property values. "The choice to live among the urban poor must include the choice to seek to be a good neighbor in our community by intentionally contributing to its well-being."[23]

The transformation of Jerusalem under Nehemiah's leadership did not stop when the wall was finished. The construction project of rebuilding the wall in and of itself was not enough to transform the city. Jerusalem "was wide and large, but the people within it were few, and no houses had been rebuilt" (Neh. 7:4). The city's population was too low, and private homes were still in ruins. In order for the positive momentum to continue Nehemiah would have to get people to move into Jerusalem.

The solution was to tithe people. "Now the leaders of the people lived in Jerusalem. And the rest of the people cast lots to bring one out of ten to live in Jerusalem the holy city, while nine out of ten remained in the other towns. And the people blessed all the men who willingly offered to live in Jerusalem" (Neh. 11:1-2). The tithing was both obligated and voluntary. Nehemiah used his political power to repopulate the city.

A community in free fall needs to address restoring hope in order to turn the situation around. Those considering fleeing the neighborhood need to be convinced that staying is a good option. Potential residents need to be shown the positive aspects of the community.

The rebuilding of the city will result in local leadership (Jer. 30:21). A local leader is invested in the community and is more likely to work for its wellbeing. A nation, city, and community must be able to keep its educated and highly skilled residents. Graduates need to be able to find fulfilling jobs if they are to stay. The future of a community is extremely uncertain when potential leaders are developed only to move away. Brain drain is a problem for communities as well as nations. In her classic, *The Death and Life of Great American Cities*, Jane Jacobs writes, "The key link in a perpetual slum is that too many people move out of it too fast—and in the meantime dream of getting out. This is the link that has to be broken if any other efforts at overcoming slums or slum life are to be of the least avail."[24] In order for a community to grow there must be a desire to stay. The problem of gentrification is solved when low-income communities naturally become mixed income because the original residents are improving their lives and choosing to stay.

The city will look and be radiant. Cities can look glamorous and attractive to people, but it is only God's glory that makes a city truly radiant. Jerusalem was attractive solely because it was the place where God chose to dwell. The migration to Jerusalem was in order to encounter God. They would see God's glory and have uncontainable joy.

While no city today can claim the title as the place of God's home, they need to be attractive in other ways. A city needs to provide employment and educational opportunities. On the neighborhood level, communities also need to be attractive. They can be attractive by offering residents affordable housing with nearby shops, employment opportunities, and strong relational bonds between neighbors. One means of engaging for transformation is to work to make the neighborhood a place where people want to be.

A repopulating city also needs to be the destination of migration. Isaiah 60:3 reveals that God's glory will shine so brightly that the nations will be attracted to the light. God and his glory will draw people to the restored city. Jerusalem will become like a lighthouse to the nations. Not for warning them of danger as a lighthouse does for ships, but for attracting the nations by its light. Everyone will want to be in God's presence in the city.

The people of God are made up of all ethnic groups. Likewise, a transforming city is one that welcomes peoples from around the world and from different social classes. Ethnic diversity is the current fad, but this is mainly limited to ethnic restaurants and specialty shops. True diversity is much more extensive and includes integrating the marginalized into the life of the city. A transforming city needs to attract both the wealthy and the poor.

Reflection and Action

1. What are the population trends in your area? (Stable, decreasing, or increasing)
2. What role can your church play in helping to repopulate an area hurt by population loss?

Chapter 19

Economic Justice: Reflections on 2 Kings 6:24-7:20

Afterward Ben-hadad king of Syria mustered his entire army and went up and besieged Samaria. And there was a great famine in Samaria, as they besieged it, until a donkey's head was sold for eighty shekels of silver, and the fourth part of a kab of dove's dung for five shekels of silver (2 Kings 6:24-25).

But Elisha said, "Hear the word of the Lord: thus says the Lord, Tomorrow about this time a seah of fine flour shall be sold for a shekel, and two seahs of barley for a shekel, at the gate of Samaria" (2 Kings 7:1).

Historical Background

The Syrian siege of Samaria came at a time when Israel and Judah were in a period of decline. Internally, they were in a downward spiral of spiritual decent as they turned away from God and worshiped the gods of neighboring nations. Idols became common in the land. They were also becoming economically polarized. Wealth began to be concentrated in the hands of an emerging elite.

Along with their internal problems they were also in a continuous war with neighboring Syria. The conflict was originally limited to border raids, but it eventually escalated to a full-scale invasion and the siege of the capital city Samaria.

Poverty Profiteers

Unjust economic structures open the door for those with power to profit from the poverty of others. Poverty profiteers take advantage of the poor's need for basic necessities to exploit their labor. One woman in my church worked all day and was paid the equivalent of one dollar, well below the legal minimum wage. She continued to work under these exploitative conditions because she felt she had no other options. A man in a home Bible study I led was paid twice a month based on a 30-day month. Every time he worked on the 31st of the month he would not be paid for that day. He could not quit because he had two children he needed to provide for.

The siege of Samaria had a devastating effect on the population. Products that were so undesirable they would normally be worthless became unaffordable. A donkey's head is edible and could be cooked with dove's dung, but it would have been unclean and therefore only eaten in desperation. The massive inflation and food shortage give only a glimpse of the destitution in Samaria. The conditions in the city were almost unimaginable. Samaria was in such dire straits that mothers were eating their children (see 2 Kings 6:26-29).

Destitute poverty means basic necessities are limited. Food is scarce and even cooking fuel can be burdensome. The other day, I passed an old man carrying a bundle of wood and a young boy not far behind dragging a large branch. These were two individuals, who instead of enjoying life at their age, were burdened by the task of finding affordable cooking fuel. Their situation did not just happen. It was created by injustice and oppression.

From the perspective of the Syrian army, the siege was working perfectly. The entire population of Samaria would eventually starve to death or surrender. Either way Syria walks away victorious without causalities.

In traditional ancient warfare, two armies facing each other in open battle limited civilian casualties. Siege warfare raised the stakes dramatically because it put the entire population at risk. History professor Paul Kern writes, "The most unconventional aspect of siege warfare was the involvement of women and children."[25] The entire population of a city suffered and faced death so the attacking army could reap the spoils of war while limiting their own losses. Siege warfare caused destitute poverty in a city in order to win a military victory without actually having to fight. It used hunger as a weapon for the benefit of the attacking army.

Widespread urban poverty has its causalities, but it also has its benefactors. Money can be made because some people suffer from poverty. One of the major reasons why it is so difficult to break poverty's grip is because some people benefit from the status quo and have no interest in changing it.

In Nehemiah's work to rebuild Jerusalem's wall, he faced opposition from poverty profiteers who were interested in keeping the status quo. Sanballat and Tobiah verbally insulted the work (Neh. 4:1-3), conspired to fight against Jerusalem (Neh. 4:7-9), slandered Nehemiah (Neh. 6:1-9), and even hired a false prophet to deceive Nehemiah (Neh. 6:10-14). Sanballat and Tobiah were there before Nehemiah's arrival and had established themselves in the region. They saw the wall of Jerusalem as a threat to their power.

One has to pose the question as to why rebuilding the wall of Jerusalem was viewed as such a threat. The most likely explanation is that Sanballat and Tobiah faced financial loss if Jerusalem was rebuilt. Christian community developer Robert Lupton theorizes that Sanballat and Tobiah controlled the trade routes that bypassed Jerusalem because the city was in ruins. This would have given them great potential to earn a lot of money. Lupton writes, "If the Judean borders were to come under the control of a strong central Jerusalem government and trading practices were legitimized, this could severely affect their lucrative cartel."[26]

The wealthy in Samaria capitalized on Jerusalem's loss, and fortunes were made. As long as Jerusalem remained in ruins their profits were secure. Once Jerusalem's walls were rebuilt the trade routes would shift back to Jerusalem and all the money with them. Sanballat, Tobiah, and the wealthy in Samaria were not going to sit back and watch their incomes drop. They actively opposed the rebuilding of Jerusalem.

Economics of Enough

Samaria during Elisha's day was completely different. In the midst of the destitution of Samaria, Elisha offers hope. With the inspiration of God, he shared his vision of the city's restoration in the form of the return of basic commodities at affordable prices. The transformation of the city of Samaria came about when God caused a great fear to come over the army of Syria. They fled in panic leaving all of their supplies in their hurried retreat. Four men with leprosy decided to surrender to the Syrians because they were so famished they thought they would die of starvation if they stayed in Samaria. When the four men entered the Syrian camp, they found it abandoned. At first, they were overcome by greed after seeing so much wealth that only they knew about. "And when these lepers came to the edge of the camp, they went into a tent and ate and drank, and they carried off silver and gold and clothing and went and hid them. Then they came back and entered another tent and carried off things from it and went and hid them" (2 Kings 7:8). Soon they realized that what they were doing was wrong. "Then they said to one another, 'We are not doing right. This day is a day of good news. If we are silent and wait until the morning light, punishment will overtake us. Now therefore come; let us go and tell the king's household'" (2 Kings 7:9). The fear of God overpowered their greed and they eventually demonstrated an economics of enough (see 2 Kings 7:1-9).

The four lepers did nothing to earn the vast hoard other than being in the right place at the right time and perhaps they were a little more desperate than everyone else in Samaria. The lepers were the first to know that the

Syrian army had fled. Reporting their find was not a great act. It is what anyone who fears God should do.

The four men with leprosy could have kept their find a secret and become very wealthy because of it. They simply would have taken advantage of a business opportunity. The Syrians left the supplies, so the four men could justify their keeping all of the wealth that they found. As long as they controlled all of the food from the Syrian camp, they could have theoretically kept the prices at inflated rates and become the dominant business leaders of the city. This would have prolonged the suffering of the average citizen, and created a situation where poverty increases during a period of economic growth. This probably would not have happened at that time, but it is not out of the range of possibilities today.

Instead of jumping on the opportunity to become the business owners of the year, the four men knew that keeping it all to themselves was wrong in the eyes of God. It was wrong because they lacked love for their neighbors who were suffering from poverty. They had nothing to do with the famine, in fact they themselves suffered more than most people in Samaria. However, when they found the abandoned camp it would have been an injustice against everyone else in Samaria to hoard all of the wealth while allowing the rest of the people to suffer from poverty. They had the resources to end the famine, so out of fear of God they did what they knew was right and reported their findings. The city of Samaria was transformed in part through an economics of enough demonstrated by the four lepers.

An economics of enough is important for transforming today's cities. Economic growth concentrated in the hands of a few can add to the hardship of the poor as policies become more and more oppressive. Businesses must have a social agenda and not simply be about maximum profits. Ajie, a businesswoman friend of mine, is a great example of owning a business that models an economics of enough. Ajie runs a burger business within her community using a business model that views other businesses as neighbors not as competitors. She knows the other shop owners and does not want to put them out of business. She is not trying to control the entire market in the community, so she avoids offering products that the shops around her sell.

As much as possible she wants to help other businesses in the neighborhood, so she orders her bread from a bakeshop a few doors away from her shop. She wants to offer her impoverished neighbors quality food at affordable prices, so her profit margin is low. Her business does make a profit, if not it would close down. But with an economics of enough, Ajie is more interested in seeing her business as a positive feature in her community than becoming rich.

Reflection and Action

1. In what ways do others benefit from poverty in your city and/or community?
2. What might it look like to practice an economics of enough in your life?
3. How can an economics of enough be integrated into your church's discipleship?

Chapter 20

Job Creation: Reflections on Jeremiah 32:36-44

I will make with them an everlasting covenant, that I will not turn away from doing good to them. And I will put the fear of me in their hearts, that they may not turn from me. I will rejoice in doing them good, and I will plant them in this land in faithfulness, with all my heart and all my soul. "For thus says the LORD: Just as I have brought all this great disaster upon this people, so I will bring upon them all the good that I promise them. Fields shall be bought in this land of which you are saying, 'It is a desolation, without man or beast; it is given into the hand of the Chaldeans.' Fields shall be bought for money, and deeds shall be signed and sealed and witnessed, in the land of Benjamin, in the places about Jerusalem, and in the cities of Judah, in the cities of the hill country, in the cities of the Shephelah, and in the cities of the Negeb; for I will restore their fortunes, declares the LORD (Jeremiah 32:40-44).

Jeremiah encouraged the exiles with the news that there will be a new and everlasting covenant. He repeats for the third time, "they shall be my people, and I will be their God" (Jer. 32:38, see also Jer. 30:22 and 31:33). To be God's people is to be in a relationship with him.

Jeremiah continually emphasized a restored relationship with God. God brought about the exile and he is now bringing about the restoration. The time before the exile they faced the violence of an enemy army. During the exile they lived as conquered people in a foreign land. Yet, under God's restoration they would dwell in safety.

Economic Participation

God commanded Jeremiah to buy a field in the midst of political uncertainty (Jer. 32:8-15). Jeremiah bought the field and then prayed about his confusion over the strange command (Jer. 32:16-25). God assured Jeremiah that nothing is impossible for him (Jer. 32:27). He will bring about judgment upon his people and city, but it will not be a complete annihilation. He will also forgive and restore them.

Jeremiah showed great faith in God when he bought a field even though the future of the nation seemed uncertain. Destruction was upon them, but it would not last. There would come a time when their fortunes would be restored. Just as Jeremiah bought a field, land will once again be bought and sold throughout the nation.

To buy and sell land is to participate in the economic system of the nation. This broad participation in the buying and selling of land meant that wealth was distributed throughout the nation. The opposite situation existed before the exile when only a few people controlled all the wealth. Isaiah warned against the elite buying up all the land. "Woe to those who join house to house, who add field to field, until there is no more room, and you are made to dwell alone in the midst of the land" (Isa. 5:8). One of the ways God used the exile was to bring an end to the wealth accumulation of the elite.

Economic participation is dependent on having the means to make purchases. There needs to be enough economic growth to provide employment for the working population. Employment also needs to pay justly in order for there to be true economic participation.

Restored Economic Wealth

The main feature of the restoration of economic wealth was that the land was once again desirable. The fields that are in desolation will once again be turned into productive farmland. Fields of rocks and weeds will be worked and planted. God will bless the fields with abundant produce creating wealth. In the agricultural economy of Israel, land was the means of production and wealth creation. With the buying and selling of land the economy would be on the road to recovery.

Isaiah also revealed a variety of economic indicators of a restored city. The city will be wealthy. It will have the abundance of the sea (Isa. 60:5), a multitude of camels (Isa. 60:6), and silver and gold will come to the city (Isa. 60:9). There will be a surplus of jobs available, so much so that immigrants come to find work (Isa. 60:10).

The Poor Overcoming Poverty

The poor overcoming poverty is usually not rags to riches. It is having stability and their basic needs met. For this to happen oppressive structures must be removed so that economic growth reaches beyond the upper classes. Just distribution of wealth does not mean that everyone has the same net worth. It means that the working population is able to keep the fruit of their labor. Fields are bought and sold. The rich are not buying up all of the available property and forcing the poor into deeper destitution.

Exodus 16 gives a picture of what God's economic system looks like. When the Israelites were in the wilderness they complained against God because they wanted food. God told Moses that he would provide food for them each day, and they were to gather exactly what they needed for that day. Those who did not listen to Moses and greedily gathered extra, ended up with smelly manna infested with maggots. Everyone within the Israelite community was to have enough to eat, and no one was to hoard by gathering more than they could use. They were to have faith that God would continue to meet their daily needs. This set the standard by which the economy of Israel was to be based.

The people of God were to live differently from the nations around them. They were not to have an elite class that owned everything while the masses lived in destitution. God provided for the basic needs of the people so that no one was famished. He prevented anyone from gathering too much so that they would not think they no longer needed God. He also ensured that everyone would have enough because God limited how much the strongest could gather. This allowed the weakest to be able to gather what they needed.

Workers need just compensation through jobs that pay livable wages. A city can have a growing economy that leaves out the poor. Economic growth is just an illusion if it leaves the poor behind. Economic participation of the poor is one way to ensure just and sustainable transformation. In order for there to be economic participation there needs to be wealth creation among the poor. This can be achieved through education and vocational skills development accompanied by job placement, as well as the creation of micro-businesses among the poor.

An Abundance of Jobs

An abundance of jobs is a key component of transformation. Economic growth is both macro and micro. Both the nation as a whole and the city need to continually create new jobs. The jobs need to be broad enough to provide employment for all sectors of society. Employment for the poor is vital. Linthicum writes, "Jobs are a priority for God in the city he desires to have for humanity. Jobs should, consequently, be a priority to the church as well."[27]

An important factor is connecting the poor to jobs. Marjorie worked as a manager at a food stall. She used her position to help others find work. Having experienced the difficulty of looking for a job, Marjorie desired to help those unemployed in her community. Whenever her boss would express the need for another employee, Marjorie would personally approach the person she had in mind to hire and offer them the job. Marjorie has helped a number of people from her community find work.

Many cities simply do not provide enough jobs, so the poor find creative solutions to create their own jobs. Informal settlements of the Majority World provide a beautiful example of the entrepreneurial poor improving their lives through starting home-based businesses. The poor cannot afford the major expenses that go into starting a new business so home-based stores that cater to neighbors must be a viable option. Microbusinesses tend not to have employees, so they do not create jobs for others, but for the sole proprietor they provide an important source of income. Self-employment is a vital lifeline for many of the world's poor.

The efforts of the poor to improve their lives should be encouraged and assisted. The simple action of turning a skill into a business can be enough to break the cycle of poverty. Sadly, this is often overlooked and even criminalized in North America by neighborhood zoning authorities. In a transforming city the entrepreneurial poor should be aided and empowered. Legislators need to rewrite land use laws for the poor to be allowed to turn their homes into businesses. Microenterprise development needs to become a priority for local governments so that funding is available for business training and grants for start-ups. [28]

Reflection and Action

1. Meet with a small business owner to discuss how your church can help small businesses in your area.
2. What can your church do to invest in the entrepreneurial poor?

Chapter 21

Food Security for Everyone: Reflections on Joel 3:17-21

> So you shall know that I am the LORD your God, who dwells in Zion, my holy mountain. And Jerusalem shall be holy, and strangers shall never again pass through it. "And in that day the mountains shall drip sweet wine, and the hills shall flow with milk, and all the streambeds of Judah shall flow with water; and a fountain shall come forth from the house of the LORD and water the Valley of Shittim (Joel 3:17-18).

Facing Food Shortages

Before I was married, I tried to live in Manila on $2 a day for ten months. This in itself was a stretch, but then a group of teenage guys decided to move in with me. It was then that I saw the horrors of chronic food shortages firsthand.

Each meal consisted of about 1 kilo of the cheapest rice available and either a bowl of ramen noodles cooked with an egg or a small can of sardines or tuna to be split among us. When there was absolutely nothing left, I watched in shock as one of the guys ate rice with a little bit of cooking oil poured on top for flavor. My concern that they were not getting enough nutrients in their meals was taken to another level when all he ate was carbohydrates and fat.

Those wealthy enough to drive to grocery stores in order to purchase food do not experience the lack of healthy food options often experienced by the poor. This is different from the food shortages of Joel's time that were caused by locusts destroying the crops. The food shortages in Joel affected the entire city, while modern food deserts are an issue of poverty.

There was a plague of locusts that devastated the land. "What the cutting locust left, the swarming locust has eaten. What the swarming locusts left, the hopping locust has eaten, and what the hopping locust left, the destroying locust has eaten" (Joel 1:4).[29] Locusts had the potential to consume an entire crop, instantly plunging the whole region into a famine.

Joel ends his message with hope of renewal. The calamity is at hand, but hope will follow because God is their refuge. God was their hope when their food supply was destroyed. He brings peace to a city devastated by food shortages.

Dietary Improvements

Joel's vision of economic prosperity is one of the fruits of holiness. The streams of the nation flow with water. The mountain vineyards are so productive with grapes that they drip sweet wine. The hills are such good pasturelands that the supply of milk seemed unlimited.

A fountain of water will flow from the temple itself. In a vision similar to Ezekiel's river of life (Ezek. 47:1-12), the house of God is shown to be the source of living water. God is the reason for the abundant supply of wine, milk, and water so that the city can feed its entire population.

Earlier in his book Joel wrote, "Be glad, O children of Zion, and rejoice in the Lord your God, for he has given the early rain for your vindication; he has poured down for you abundant rain, the early and the latter rain, as before. The threshing floors shall be full of grain; the vats shall overflow with wine and oil" (Joel 2:23-24). The imagery in Joel is not excessive consumerism of greed but good quality food and water to spare. They will eat their fill and praise God.

A transforming community results in a new mealtime question for the city's poor. They no longer ask, "Will there be dinner?" Rather they will ask, "What's for dinner?" Not knowing when your next meal will be is a painful experience. Small portions need to get shared among family members and stretched for several meals. The result is chronic hunger and all the negative health and emotional effects that go along with it.

The food of the poor is not only limited in quantity, but also in quality. There is not enough food for the household, and the food that is available and affordable is unhealthy. The kind of food you eat matters. Packaged processed food is often cheaper and much more readily available than fresh fruits and vegetables.

Having enough food to eat meets the problem of chronic hunger but sometimes contributes to future health problems because of the low quality diet. Isabel Carter writes, "A healthy diet is directly linked to good health. It is particularly important for pregnant women, babies and young children. Well-nourished babies and children are much less likely to become sick through disease and infection."[30] A healthy diet is just as important as having enough to eat.

The only way nutritional needs can be met is when healthy food options are accessible and affordable. Fresh fruits and vegetables need to be real options when grocery shopping. Real fruit needs to be just as available and cheap as processed fruit flavored junk food.

Food deserts, where people in certain neighborhoods do not have access to healthy food options, are a policy issue created by zoning laws and community design. Food deserts do not exist in cities where the poor are allowed to sell fresh produce from their home. Eliminating these legal hurdles will go a long way in greatly reducing food deserts.

Transforming communities have improved diets for the residents. For this to happen the poorest residents need to be able to afford enough healthy food for the entire household. There also needs to be food justice at the city, national, and global levels. Fresh fruits and vegetables need to be available in low-income communities at affordable prices across the planet.

I have a friend who is engaged in her community by working to help improve the diet of her neighbors. She began working with the children to show them how to grow vegetables in pots that could be placed in their windowsills and rooftops. The idea caught on and many of the families started windowsill vegetable gardens. Although the quantity is limited, they at least have some fresh vegetables to supplement their diet.

Aside from the negative effects on health, another issue caused by food deserts is that produce becomes unrecognizable and the residents do not know how to cook using fresh ingredients. Andrew, a social entrepreneur with a vision to address the issues of urban food deserts, opened With Love Market and Café in a multicultural mixed-income community in South Los Angeles. He wants to give the residents of his community the option to eat good quality, healthy, and affordable food. In light of this, With Love Market and Café only sells positive or neutral foods. They do not sell much of the junk food that is normally a standard in most stores in their neighborhood. This results in a lower bottom line but allows them to have a positive impact on their community.

When With Love Market and Café opened they struggled to sell affordable produce and began to question, why people don't buy produce? They discovered that the issue is deeper than simply the lack of affordable fresh produce. The working poor juggling two jobs simply do not have time to cook. There is also the issue of knowing how to cook with fresh produce. That resulted in teaching weekly bilingual cooking classes. The classes are offered at different times of the day and different days of the week to make them as available as possible. One monthly series was called From the Ground Up and focused on cooking with grains. Another series was on healthy snacks. They have also offered kids' cooking classes catering to local students.

After offering classes on cooking with certain products there is an increase in sales of that product. Those who attend the classes are trying out the new recipes. Healthy food options are being made available, and just as importantly the residents are learning cooking skills needed to eat healthier.

While I was hanging out in With Love Market and Café, a homeless man walked in asking other customers for money. As I observed he was given some cash and a gift card, but more strikingly he was spoken to as a human being. The employees did not kick him out as a nuisance. With Love Market and Café truly did live up to its name.[31]

Reflection and Action

1. What can your church do to ensure that the poor in your community have access to fresh, healthy, and affordable food options?
2. Identify the food deserts in your city.

Chapter 22

Housing for Everyone: Reflections on Isaiah 4:2-6

In that day the branch of the LORD shall be beautiful and glorious, and the fruit of the land shall be the pride and honor of the survivors of Israel. And he who is left in Zion and remains in Jerusalem will be called holy, everyone who has been recorded for life in Jerusalem, when the Lord shall have washed away the filth of the daughters of Zion and cleansed the bloodstains of Jerusalem from its midst by a spirit of judgment and by a spirit of burning. Then the LORD will create over the whole site of Mount Zion and over her assemblies a cloud by day, and smoke and the shining of a flaming fire by night; for over all the glory there will be a canopy. There will be a booth for shade by day from the heat, and for a refuge and a shelter from the storm and rain (Isaiah 4:2-6).

Isaiah's vision of the restored city of Jerusalem is directly connected to the wider context of God's judgment in chapter 3. Burning signified God's judgment upon the city. Fire will purify the city and cleanse its bloodstains so that the remnant will be holy.

Isaiah makes a third reference to "in that day" or the day of the Lord. Isaiah's use of "in that day" from 3:10 and 4:1 is on judgment, but in 4:2-6 the focus is on redemption. God will restore the city and be its protection from the heat and a shelter from the storm. Using symbolism from the wandering years following the exodus, Isaiah envisions the restored Jerusalem as the destination of the journey.

In the wilderness after the Hebrews were delivered from slavery in Egypt the cloud and fire were used by God to guide them where he wanted them to go (see Exod. 13:21-22). In Isaiah the cloud and fire are God's protection over the city. God's people were no longer traveling so they did not need to know which way to go. However, they were vulnerable and needed God's protection. He was their shelter from the elements.

The three main features of Isaiah's message are: the fruit of the land will be the pride and honor of the survivors, those who remain in Jerusalem shall be called holy, and God's presence will be seen through being a shelter for Jerusalem. In order for the fruit of the land to be a pride for the residents it must be productive. After all, it's giant produce that wins the county fair, not a blighted crop. The land surrounding the restored city would become productive, resulting in the recovery of the economic system. The people of God experienced a spiritual revival as they began to live in obedience. The judgment of sin is over and there is a renewed desire to walk in holiness. Lastly, God's presence is manifested as a shelter for the city.

A Transforming City Provides Shelter for all its Residence

In the glorified Jerusalem God himself will create a tent to provide shade from the sun and shelter from storms. The residents of the glorified city were given two levels of protection: a tent and a canopy. God himself provided protection from the elements of nature. Everyone in the city was safe from the heat and from the rain.

The elite living in palaces did not need protection from the heat and storms. It was Jerusalem's poor that knew the misery of hot days. They were also all too familiar with how deadly nature can be when one is exposed to the elements. Protection from the heat and storms is a felt need of the poor.

The poor in general live in areas that are vulnerable to natural disasters simply because that is where they can afford to live. The poor living in informal settlements and tent cities are often forced to build their homes on floodplains because that is the only place the authorities do not harass them. This makes them especially vulnerable to storms. I visited a community in Manila located right next to a stream. Every time it rained the stream flooded. The homes were all two stories and almost nothing was kept on the first floor because it had to be carried to the second floor whenever it rained.

Storms can greatly add to the hardship of the poor. Whole communities can be destroyed in an instant. For the poor rebuilding is always difficult. A natural disaster can immediately wipe out one's life savings. On top of the financial difficulties, governments often use storms as an opportunity to remove the poor from areas where they are not wanted. Governments prevent rebuilding using the excuse that the area is unsafe even though it was government policy that forced the poor out of all the other viable locations in the first place.

The most vulnerable segment of a city's population to the heat, cold, and storms are the homeless. Informal settlers at least have homes that provide protection from the elements. The homeless are completely exposed.

Communities must address homelessness holistically. Linthicum writes, "The church is to work for adequate housing for all, so that everyone has a home and no one is forced to live on the street."[32] Homeless shelters are important for providing temporary housing for the homeless, but other issues must be addressed simultaneously. Affordable housing, livable wage employment, education, health care, and services for mental illness all need to be in place.

The shortage of affordable housing is one of the chronic problems cities face. Affordable housing is not available because real estate developers can make more money building homes for the upper classes as opposed to small inexpensive homes. Housing is one area that cannot be left to market forces. Government regulation is needed to ensure that everyone has housing options.

Local governments need to make affordable housing a top priority. Montgomery writes, "Governments must step in with subsidized social housing, rent controls, initiatives for housing cooperatives, or other policy measures."[33] They need to come alongside the poor in their efforts to address the shortage of affordable housing. The church must engage politically to ensure that policy makers actually work for housing for all.

Housing for low-income families should not only provide shelter and security, but also help the residents overcome poverty. This can be done through learning how the poor build their own communities. Informal settlements are naturally mixed-use, mixed-income, and walkable. City planners and politicians must adopt these qualities in order to address the issue of affordable housing. A community that is mixed-use allows the entrepreneurial poor to start businesses from their homes and enables the poor to purchase basic goods without having to spend extra money on transportation. Mixed-income communities help create vibrant areas where young graduates want to stay. These communities also allow for a variety of business opportunities to thrive in a diverse environment. Walkable neighborhoods free the poor from needing to purchase a car to survive. A neighborhood that is able to blend these three characteristics is one that helps the poor improve their lives and overcome poverty.

The greatest builders of affordable housing that meets the needs of the poor are the poor themselves. Across the globe, the poor build millions of homes. These homes are built with local talent using local materials. Most importantly they are built specifically to meet the needs of the poor.

The presence of informal settlements and tent cities exposes the injustice of governments favoring the wealthy at the expense of the poor. Faced with a shortage of affordable housing, the poor create their own solution by building their own communities. More often than not, they do so while facing opposition from the power holders. This is because cities tend to crush the efforts of the poor to build their own affordable houses. Instead of being the focus of demolition and harassment, informal settlements and tent cities should be assisted with government services.

Informal settlements and tent cities help the poor improve their lives. This is why the poor fight the demolition of their homes in informal settlements and do not necessarily make it their life goal to move out. In contrast, the residents in government housing projects have the social pressure to move out as soon as possible. Rich city planners, architects, and politicians are usually unaware of the day-to-day realities of poverty. Meeting the needs of the poor also rarely makes the top ten list of objectives for affordable housing. It should be no surprise that government housing projects suck the life out of the residents. Thankfully a better option is available. That is to design communities directly around the needs of the poor with the goal of helping them overcome poverty.[34]

Reflection and Action

1. What can you and your church do to work for more affordable housing in your community?
2. What would it take for communities in your area to be built with the specific goal of helping the poor overcome poverty?
3. Have a meal with a homeless person and try to learn their story.

Chapter 23

Restored Health: Reflections on Jeremiah 33:1-16

Behold, I will bring to it health and healing, and I will heal them and reveal to them abundance of prosperity and security. I will restore the fortunes of Judah and the fortunes of Israel, and rebuild them as they were at first. I will cleanse them from all the guilt of their sin against me, and I will forgive all the guilt of their sin and rebellion against me. And this city shall be to me a name of joy, a praise and a glory before all the nations of the earth who shall hear of all the good that I do for them. They shall fear and tremble because of all the good and all the prosperity I provide for it (Jeremiah 33:6-9).

Jerusalem faced certain defeat. Death and destruction were all around. Jeremiah knew that the situation was going to get worse before it got better. The Babylonian army would eventually breach the city's wall, take the survivors into exile, and burn what remained of the city. Jerusalem was quickly becoming a wasteland.

In a situation of gloom, Jeremiah offered a message of hope for the distant future. Health and healing would eventually come to a broken people. God will cleanse their sins and bring healing, as part of the holistic restoration of the nation. The city's fortunes will be returned, bringing with it an abundance of prosperity and security. Celebrations will be heard as the people sing praise to God.

Health and Healing

One of the pains of poverty is the negative effect on health. Children and seniors are the most vulnerable to the risks of living without access to affordable healthcare. The two-year-old daughter of my neighbor was taken to the hospital when intestinal worms crawled up her throat and out of her mouth. She was given medication, which killed the parasites. Almost immediately she began to gain weight and no longer suffered chronic fevers. If the family had the financial means to take their daughter to the doctor before it was a medical emergency, she could have been cured much earlier. By God's mercy the child survived, but many do not.

Gloom and despair are not final. God cares for the welfare of his people and brings the city health and healing. Old Testament scholar Walter Brueggemann writes, "The creator of heaven and earth is the God who assured attentiveness to and care for the exiles. The God of all power is the God who attends to the powerless. The God who seemed to be absent is present, findable, and approachable."[35] God's power and availability are hope for healing in the restored city.

A transforming community must be a place where its residents can maintain health. Linthicum writes, "The city is to be a place of health, and the church has the responsibility to work for the longevity and health care of its inhabitants."[36] Restored health is foundational for the overall wellbeing of a community. Sicknesses are financial burdens for households. The more households have to deal with medical problems, the more work and school absences will pile up, undercutting a family's ability to improve their lives. Medical bills can cause years of debt pushing families deeper and deeper into destitution. They will also be less involved in solving community issues. A neighborhood that is lowering the health problems of the residents has more residents that are better able to participate in the local economy and improve the community.

Working for restored health includes a wide array of approaches depending on the needs, skills, and resources available. Providing medical services, medicine, advocacy, and health education are all important aspects of restored health. The way that my church has been engaged to promote restored health in our community is through athletics.

Sport and Development

Involvement in sports is one way to improve the overall health of a community. The growing field of sport and development uses sports as a means of holistic development. Sports can help develop life skills such as resilience, dedication, teamwork, coping with pressure, and physical fitness. Sports are also a great way to teach health education.

Sports have been useful in a variety of developmental fields. Sport and development professors Roger Levermore and Aaron Beacom write,

> Projects involving sport have included attempts to educate young people to appreciate health concerns (such as the dangers of HIV and malaria), engender respect for local communities, discourage anti-social and criminal behavior, increase gender-awareness, as well as assist with the rehabilitation of people with disabilities and the reconciliation of communities in conflict.[37]

Sports have great potential to bring health and healing to lives and the transformation of communities. I have been active in various sports throughout my life. As a child, involvement in sports was very beneficial. Growing up I had no interest in school. It was my involvement in baseball and wrestling that motivated me to pay attention in class, do my homework, and avoid getting into trouble. I struggled in school, so being a good athlete motivated me to put more effort into my studies. The resilience I developed as a teenager through sports helped me to complete my doctoral studies as an adult.

Our church is walking distance from a major university. Every summer we would go there to play Ultimate Frisbee as part of some of our youth services. Many of the youth liked playing so we joined an interchurch tournament. In the weeks leading up to the tournament we got serious about training and practiced regularly.

Our first match in the tournament was against a team with flashy uniforms. We were a rag-tag group of teenagers and young adults from an informal settlement. Some of our players did not even have proper shoes much less cleats. I prayed that we would at least score so it would not be a total blowout. The opposing team took an early lead, but as the game progressed they ran out of steam and we were able to clinch a victory. That really fired our players up. They fought their way to the championship but lost in the final seconds. The players were happy with a surprise second place, so our church organized an Ultimate team.

One of the players who began to distinguish himself as a leader was Joker. Being a naturally gifted athlete, Joker quickly developed the basic skills of the game and began to improve. As his confidence grew, he began joining pick-up games at the university. This opened the door for him to build friendships with students and professors. His new friends encouraged him to enroll in college. Our church was able to help secure a scholarship for Joker thanks to generous donations from Servant Partners interns. By the grace of God, Joker was able to pursue university studies.

I began working with Joker to help him develop as a coach. Together we took an online course on sport and development and learned how to use athletics beyond merely a gimmick to get teens to come to our youth service. We applied what we learned from that course and began to intentionally integrate athletics to life skills they need off the field. Joker and I put together a life skills playbook where we listed different life skills we want our players to grow in and reflection questions to go with each life skill. During practices we are able to debrief both the Ultimate drill and the specific life skill simultaneously. The players are gaining athletic skills as well as skills for life such as teamwork, people skills, and accountability.

Joker is great with relationships and he started reaching out to the young teens in the neighborhood by inviting them to play Ultimate. One of the high school students that joined the team was Anndrea. She is a natural athlete and picked up Ultimate quickly to become one of our top female players. Playing Ultimate helps her to relieve stress and stay fit. Playing has taught her how to work as a team and to enjoy the game even if she loses. As her playing skills continue to improve, she has gained confidence as a person. Although she is still in high school, she joined a tournament for college players. Her playing was so impressive that she was given an honorable mention award for being a young player able to compete at the college level.

Her involvement in Ultimate has helped her to meet a lot of new friends, particularly older college students, professors, and young professionals. This network of professionals has allowed Anndrea to break out of the isolation of poverty. These networks have the potential to open up study or employment opportunities in the future.

Reflection and Action

1. Based on the overall health care services for the poor, how just is your city?
2. What role can sport and development play in helping your community become a healthier place to live?

Section IV

Practical Ministry

Chapter 24

Leadership for Rebuilding Ruined Cities: Reflections on Ezra and Nehemiah

> They finished their building by decree of the God of Israel (Ezra 6:14).

Ezra and Nehemiah served in Jerusalem as a priest and politician. Their combined efforts helped finally rebuild Jerusalem after it sat in ruins for over a century. They provided the leadership needed to rebuild their city.

Ezra: Spiritual Leader as Urban Rebuilder

Spiritual leadership is needed to point people toward God as they experience their neighborhood improving. For as long as we have been in Botocan, the community has been in a season of renewal. Both private residents and the local government are working to improve the neighborhood. The residents have an overall sense of hope about their neighborhood. Violence has decreased, there are now employment opportunities, and people are generally hopeful. They are seeing the fruit of their effort to improve their lives. Private homes are being upgraded and cottage businesses are flourishing. The local government has also had a few successful projects such as hiring full-time security guards and the continual improvement of the underground drainage system.

In the midst of the physical transformation that was already happening, the Holy Spirit was at work. Faith Gospel Community (FGC), the other church in Botocan, experienced a time a rapid growth and began holding multiple services. We planted Botocan Bible Christian Fellowship and also felt the blessing of the Holy Spirit. Many gifted leaders committed their lives to Christ and served in our church.

Since our church was planted at a time when the community was experiencing positive transformation, we were able to ride the momentum of what God was already doing in the community. There was a lot of interest when we began teaching the Bible. Many people committed their lives to follow Jesus and became active in our church.

About one year after we launched our new church, Charisse came to help start our youth service. She is a gifted leader and worked to build the foundations of our youth ministry. One of the keys to Charisse's impact was her passion to see people come to faith in Christ and walk in obedience to Scripture. Charisse organized several summer programs that were well attended. She organized a youth outing in partnership with FGC that was so well attended we were stopped for protesting without a permit. We actually did look like a protest because it was a huge group of youth walking down the street. I had to go to an official's office and explain that we were not protesters.

Ezra was passionate about the spiritual purity of the people. He knew all too well that the city and temple were destroyed and the people were taken into exile because they had turned from God. Ezra was committed to making sure that would not happen again.

Faithful servants of God need to be committed to studying and teaching the Bible. "For Ezra had set his heart to study the Law of the LORD, and to do it and to teach his statutes and rules in Israel" (Ezra 7:10). Ezra was faithfully committed to serving as the spiritual leader of the people. Studying the Law of God and teaching Scripture was a central part of his ministry. Ezra's role in rebuilding the city was to know, obey, and teach the Bible.

Spiritual leadership is needed for urban transformation. We need a constant reminder to point to God as the source of all restoration. Spiritual leaders have the vital role of proclaiming God's reign. They also need to encourage the people of God to love others in practical ways.

Spiritual leadership provides a prophetic voice for the marginalized. On the grassroots level this includes developing a critical consciousness by helping people to see the injustices within their communities. It also includes holding those in power accountable for their actions that hurt others.

Nehemiah: Political Leader as Urban Rebuilder

Nehemiah provided the political leadership needed to rebuild. He had the vision and political power necessary to complete the task. Nehemiah was intentional about rebuilding Jerusalem. His request to the king was for permission to go to Jerusalem to rebuild (Neh. 2:5). The city sat in ruins for generations so Nehemiah must have realized that nothing was going to change unless someone stepped up and acted.

Nehemiah used his political skills to motivate the people to begin the work of rebuilding the city's wall (Neh. 2:17-18). The King of Persia had given him authority to rebuild the city's wall so he could have simply dictated that order upon the people. Instead he chose to take his time so that the rebuilding would be participatory.

Nehemiah spent three days visiting the city and probably talking with key leaders before he finally announced the reason he was in Jerusalem. Nehemiah challenged the people by focusing on the unacceptable situation of the destroyed wall and the vulnerability of the city. Nehemiah was able to help the people to see that the city wall can and should be rebuilt.

The rebuilding of the wall was a community effort (Neh. 3). Nehemiah listed the different families and groups of people who worked on the wall. People from a wide variety of professions from goldsmiths to perfumers all came together to rebuild the wall. Even the daughters of an official in Jerusalem helped construct the wall. Female construction workers might not be out-of-the-ordinary today, but in the male dominated ancient Near East, having women join the work is a remarkable demonstration of the community effort that went into rebuilding the wall.

Nehemiah's engagement for transformation did not stop when the wall-building project was complete. That was an important part in the restoration of Jerusalem, but it was not the only thing that needed to be done. Nehemiah continued to serve the city for decades. He confronted injustices, helped repopulate the city, and worked to get the people to obey and worship God.

Leadership is a key part of a community's transformation. Political leaders have an important role in the restoration of a community. Of course, politicians can be corrupt, but they can also be visionary leaders that help bring about lasting improvements for the entire area under their authority.

Reflection and Action

1. What can you do to grow as a leader?
2. Who are the main religious and political leaders in your community or city?
3. Pray for your community's leaders.

Chapter 25

Incarnational Leadership: Reflections on Jeremiah 29:1-23

> Thus says the LORD of hosts, the God of Israel, to all the exiles whom I have sent into exile from Jerusalem to Babylon: Build houses and live in them; plant gardens and eat their produce. Take wives and have sons and daughters; take wives for your sons, and give your daughters in marriage, that they may bear sons and daughters; multiply there, and do not decrease. But seek the welfare of the city where I have sent you into exile, and pray to the LORD on its behalf, for in its welfare you will find your welfare (Jeremiah 29:4-7).

Jeremiah's letter to the exiles was most likely written soon after the fall of Jerusalem when the first group of exiles were taken into captivity. He challenged the exiles to live meaningfully in Babylon and to work for its transformation. The combined actions of living meaningfully and engaging for transformation are the definition of incarnational leadership.[38]

Jeremiah's letter was liberating. In it the exiles were freed from hatred, the need to see Babylon destroyed, and self-pity. This freedom was found in the command to build houses, plant gardens, have families, and pray for Babylon.

Living Meaningfully

"I'm dead!" This was the first thought that came to my mind as a muscular gang member strode toward me. Covered in tattoos and sipping on a beer with a group of fellow gangsters, he looked extremely intimidating.

I had recently met a guy who lived in another section of my community. He had a pet baby python and I wanted to show my three-year-old son the snake. Once we turned the corner to get to his house about six gang members blocked the walkway. If I knew they were there I would not have gone that way. The man who owned the snake was standing in his doorway and we spoke casually for a moment. He told me he had given the baby python away. I turned to make a hasty exit and noticed that all the gangsters were looking at me. One gang member stepped toward me. Expecting the worst, I almost ran away. Anxiety took over my whole body. My stomach knotted up and I broke out into a sweat.

Instead of being threatened he simply said, "Thank you." Those words were so unexpected I almost dropped my son. Still uneasy about the situation, the only thing I could say was "Why?"

He replied, "Thank you for living here and for bringing Americans to visit so they can see how we live. What you're doing is good." I thanked him and added that I liked living there. After our brief conversation I headed on my way.

The fear in the moment was transformed into praise. I thought I was just going to show my son a snake and return home, but God had other plans. Friendly encounters with gangsters don't happen every day. God was behind this encounter. My walk home became a spontaneous prayer walk praising God for his protection and for my neighbors.

This experience was a powerful reminder of the importance of living where you serve. Jeremiah's letter was a call for the exiles to start serving where they lived. They were to be incarnational leaders in Babylon by living meaningfully and engaging the city for transformation.

The actual letter to the exiles begins with Jeremiah stressing the authority of the letter as a message from God. God is shown to be "the LORD of hosts" and "the God of Israel" (Jer. 29:4). The letter emphasizes that God sent the exiles from Jerusalem to Babylon, making it clear that they were exactly where God wanted them to be. This is repeated four times in the letter: Jeremiah 29:4, 7, 14, and 20. It was by God's sovereign design that his people were physically present in Babylon. Everything the Israelites were to do in Babylon was connected to their location. God intended for both the Israelites and the city of Babylon to be transformed through the presence of the Israelites living there.

The Israelites were political prisoners taken to Babylon by force, yet they were not locked away in prison. They were given the freedom to live meaningfully in Babylon, but at first they chose not to. They were not on a temporary excursion even though they were living like it. Jeremiah confronts this misconception and states clearly that the exile will last for seventy years (Jer. 29:10).

Since they were going to be there for the rest of their lives, Jeremiah explained how the Israelites should live in Babylon. They were to "Build houses and live in them; plant gardens and eat their produce. Take wives and have sons and daughters; take wives for your sons, and give your daughters in marriage, that they may bear sons and daughters; multiply there, and do not decrease" (Jer. 29:5-6). The three components of this command were to have a home, a job, and a family. They were to live meaningfully in Babylon. Their lives were to be interconnected with the city. They were to have investments in the form of homes and gardens. Their mindset would be changed, and they would no longer desire the destruction of Babylon, because if it were destroyed, their investments would also be destroyed.

Having a meaningful relationship is beyond high fives and hellos. It does not mean having celebrity type popularity. It means building loving and trusting relationships.

Engaging a Community for Transformation

Engagement flows out of a meaningful presence. Bob Ekbald, co-director of Tierra Nueva, writes, "Ministry of presence is a way of living out God's unconditional love and respect by coming alongside people, connecting with them personally, demonstrating solidarity and tender care through humbly being with them in the midst of their lives, and engaging with them based on their felt needs."[39] Jeremiah's letter to the exiles modeled engagement rooted in a meaningful presence.

Living meaningfully in Babylon was not enough. The exiles were also to engage the city for transformation. They were to seek Babylon's welfare and pray for the city (Jer. 29:7). The Israelites were already to "pray for the peace of Jerusalem!" (Ps. 122:6). Now that they were in Babylon, they were to pray for that city. Praying for Babylon was their act of engagement. Integrating faith in urban transformation is the process of journeying with your neighbors through relationships and engagement.

Engagement in one's community can take hundreds of different forms. It can include church planting, Bible studies, sport and development, microfinance, food justice, public safety, community organizing, and a whole array of activities that make the community a better place to live. Regardless of how we are engaged, the relational factor is always important. This is why engagement goes hand in hand with a meaningful presence.

God uses incarnational leaders as agents of transformation in cities today. Neighborhoods left in ruins by oppression and neglect will not be transformed from the outside regardless of how well funded programs are. Local leaders need to stop moving out, and others committed to the neighborhood need to move in. Bakke writes, "We are not going to change the slums unless some of us take the relocation of our human resources seriously."[40]

I have lived in informal settlements as a single, married without children, and married with children. Both of my boys grew up in an informal settlement. There has been pain and suffering as well as great joy in the work of the Holy Spirit in my community. God used our presence in our community to start a church that is seeing people come to faith and their lives transformed.

We first met Rose when she was twelve years old. At that time, she was on the verge of dropping out of school. Her school attendance was literally a few days a month. On a good week she would go to school three days. She was emotionally and physically neglected at home. No one cared if she went to school or not. The family did not have enough to feed everyone, so Rose was always hungry.

Rose came over one evening and stood in our doorway. My wife Emma chatted with her a bit, but she just kept standing there until it was awkward. I could tell she wanted to say something, but she just stood there. Finally, Emma asked her if she had eaten. Rose replied that she had not eaten all day. Emma set a plate for her and she quickly finished everything. Emma invited her to have all her dinners with us. For the next several years, Rose ate with us almost every day.

The frequency of our interaction with Rose allowed Emma to deeply invest in her. They studied the Bible and prayed together, each growing closer to Jesus in the process. As Rose matured, she faced more and more temptations. Her three closest friends all became pregnant. Her faith in Jesus and Emma's constant love and support have helped her to resist peer pressure.

When Rose graduated from high school, college seemed like an impossible dream. An internship team staying with us at the time committed to helping cover some of Rose's tuition costs. Another friend was able to raise enough money to offer Rose a full college scholarship. During her last semester of college, Rose was offered a good government job.

Although she now earns enough to live the life of a young middle-class hipster, Rose has chosen to continue to live in Botocan. She wants to invest in at-risk teens to give them the hope that she has in Jesus.

Reflection and Action

1. How are you investing in relationships in your community?
2. What ways can you be engaged for transformation?

Chapter 26

Praying for Transformation: Reflections on Daniel 9:1-19

O Lord, according to all your righteous acts, let your anger and your wrath turn away from your city Jerusalem, your holy hill, because for our sins, and for the iniquities of our fathers, Jerusalem and your people have become a byword among all who are around us. Now therefore, O our God, listen to the prayer of your servant and to his pleas for mercy, and for your own sake, O Lord, make your face to shine upon your sanctuary, which is desolate. O my God, incline your ear and hear. Open your eyes and see our desolations, and the city that is called by your name. For we do not present our pleas before you because of our righteousness, but because of your great mercy. O Lord, hear; O Lord, forgive. O Lord, pay attention and act. Delay not, for your own sake, O my God, because your city and your people are called by your name (Daniel 9:16-19).

Historical Setting of Daniel

The time period given by Daniel in 9:1-2 suggests that his prayer was at the end of the Babylonian exile. The time had come for the fulfillment of

Jeremiah's prophecy that the exile would end after seventy years (Jer. 29:10). With the fall of their captors all but guaranteed, hopes were high that the exile might finally be over.

Daniel would have been an old man by this point in his life. A life of faithfulness molded him into a passionate intercessor. His prayer was for God's glory in urban transformation. Daniel's prayer reveals his love for God and others as he asks God to work his righteousness in rebuilding Jerusalem.

God's judgment on Jerusalem was not the single event of the Babylonian army sacking and burning the city. Jerusalem was to lie in ruins throughout the entire 70-year exile, plus another 80 years until Nehemiah completed the wall.

Daniel 6 records the well-known story of King Darius being tricked into making a temporary law forbidding prayer to anyone but him. "When Daniel knew that the document had been signed, he went to his house where he had windows in his upper chamber open toward Jerusalem. He got down on his knees three times a day and prayed and gave thanks before his God, as he had done previously" (Daniel 6:10). Daniel's prayer in chapter 9 could be an example of Daniel's daily prayers.

Daniel's Prayer

Daniel 9 begins by setting the context of the prayer, followed by an introduction and the prayer itself. Daniel's prayer is mainly a confession and pleading with God to relent from his judgment upon Jerusalem. Daniel desires God's mercy upon the ruined nation and city in order to bring restoration.

Daniel starts from a posture of mourning because of the sins of the people of God. He fasts and sits in sackcloth and ashes. His experience has troubled his heart and he turns his burdens over to God in prayer.

Daniel's prayer reveals a lifetime of reading and meditating on Scripture. He understood Jeremiah's prophesy and it led him to pray. His prayer reflects on numerous parts of Scripture. Deuteronomy, 1 Kings 8, Psalms, and Jeremiah are alluded to in Daniel's prayer. Daniel poured his heart out to God with an open Bible.

The main components of Daniel's prayer are worship, confession, and requests. Daniel's prayer begins with God. Daniel worships God for who he is. God is great and awesome. He is loving and faithful to his part of the covenant.

Daniel was deeply aware that the exile was the result of God's judgment upon the nation. Daniel does not attempt to soften the reality of the nation's sin. He uses words such as "acted wickedly" and "rebelled" to describe their sin.

They are not the light of the world, as they should be. Instead they are scorned. Daniel seeks God's mercy upon Jerusalem. He prays for the transformation of Jerusalem, and the rebuilding of the temple. He asks God to change his attitude toward Jerusalem, to no longer judge the city but to look upon the city with favor. Daniel pleads with God to forgive, hear, and act. He appeals to God's mercy and the repentance of the people. Daniel's prayer of worship, confession, and requests can guide how we pray for our communities.

Prayer for Transformation

Daniel's prayer is a great challenge to continually be in the Word. Both Scripture and the current state of our city and community should inform our prayers. The rhythm of action/reflection is a useful description of the process. As we reflect on Scripture our engagement for transformation and prayers become more fine-tuned and aligned with God's plan for our communities.

Prayer for the transformation of our communities is in alignment with the example set before us by Daniel. Linthicum writes, "Scripture instructs us to pray for the economic, legal, political, and social well-being of our city and for individual relationships with God. Praying about the issues of our city, our community, and our neighborhood will have a transforming impact not only upon the social order but also upon our lives and our ministry in the city."⁴¹ Holistic prayer has a holistic impact on us as well as our communities.

There are intercessors constantly in prayer for Jerusalem, like the city's watchmen are always on guard (Isa. 62:6). God has set the intercessors, and he desires their prayers for his work in the city. The prayers are within God's will as Isaiah states God's promises to restore the city.

The founder of Philadelphia, William Penn (1644-1718), prayed for his newly founded city. It is posted on a plaque in Philadelphia's City Hall. His prayer reads:

> And thou Philadelphia the virgin settlement of this province named before thou were born what love what care what service and what travail have there been to bring thee forth and preserve thee from such as would abuse and defile thee. O that thou mayest be kept from the evil that would overwhelm thee that faithful to the God of thy mercies in the life of righteousness thou mayest be preserved to the end. My soul prays to God for thee that thou mayest stand in the day of trial that thy children may be blest of the Lord and thy people saved by his power.

William Penn's prayer for Philadelphia rightly focuses on the need to remain faithful to God. He prays for God to preserve them during trials that they may stand firm. Lastly, he prays that future generations in Philadelphia will be blessed and experience salvation through Jesus.

Praying for the transformation of our communities is an important role of local churches. Prayer builds bonds with those seeking to see their communities transformed for God's glory. Prayer for a city can help orient the people of God towards Jesus, and help them repent in times of wandering from God. Henri Nouwen writes, "By prayer, community is created as well as expressed. Prayer is first of all the realization of God's presence in the midst of his people and, therefore, the realization of the community itself."⁴² Intercession for our communities is not simply to build the internal community of the church. It is asking God to change our communities.

Praying for the transformation of my community started with a prayer for God to lead the residents to worship Jesus. I also asked God to enable us to start a new church that would love Jesus and love our neighbors. I prayed this prayer almost every time I walked through the community when we were still working on planting a church.

Reflection and Action

1. Write a prayer of worship, confession, and requests for your city.
2. Spend time in prayer for your city.

Chapter 27

Repentance and Transformation: Reflections on Jonah 3

Then the word of the LORD came to Jonah the second time, saying, "Arise, go to Nineveh, that great city, and call out against it the message that I tell you." So Jonah arose and went to Nineveh, according to the word of the LORD. Now Nineveh was an exceedingly great city, three days' journey in breadth. Jonah began to go into the city, going a day's journey. And he called out, "Yet forty days, and Nineveh shall be overthrown!" And the people of Nineveh believed God. They called for a fast and put on sackcloth, from the greatest of them to the least of them. The word reached the king of Nineveh, and he arose from his throne, removed his robe, covered himself with sackcloth, and sat in ashes. And he issued a proclamation and published through Nineveh, "By the decree of the king and his nobles: Let neither man nor beast, herd nor flock, taste anything. Let them not feed or drink water, but let man and beast be covered with sackcloth, and let them call out mightily to God. Let everyone turn from his evil way and from the violence that is in his hands. Who knows? God may turn and relent and turn from his fierce anger, so that we may not perish." When God saw what they did, how they turned from their evil way, God relented of the disaster that he had said he would do to them, and he did not do it (Jonah 3).

The book of Jonah does not provide a date for when the events took place. However, Jonah most likely went to Nineveh during the time when Assyria's future was uncertain. Nineveh was a powerful city, but also plagued with problems.

Preaching Repentance in a Megacity

God commanded Jonah to go to the city of Nineveh to warn them of his coming judgment. This act in itself showed God's love for Nineveh. Jonah, however, did not share God's concern, so he disobeyed by heading in the opposite direction. Bakke writes of Jonah, "He had no love for Israel's enemy, and he understood that God didn't love those folks either. He did not want to see the gospel preached in the Assyrian city of Nineveh after all they had done against his people."[43] Chapter 3 begins with Jonah lying on the beach in fish vomit. This time he submits to the will of God and goes to the hated city of Nineveh.

God called Nineveh a great city four times in the book of Jonah (Jonah 1:2, 3:2, 3:3, 4:11). Nineveh was a great city in the eyes of God. Perhaps it was because of the size of its population. The population was at least 120,000, a staggering number at the time.[44] The city itself was also large, especially if Jonah 3:3 is interpreted as requiring three days to walk the entire city. While the actual size of Nineveh during the time of Jonah is debated, the point is that it was a megacity at the time. God cared enough about this great city to send a prophet to preach repentance in order to prevent its destruction.

Jonah's message, "Yet forty days, and Nineveh shall be overthrown!" (Jonah 3:4), was a warning, not an unchangeable prediction of the future.

He warned them of the consequences of continuing on the path they were on. The message itself does not provide a way to stop the judgment, but by the actions of the people they understood that repentance could save their city.

Jonah preached a very brief message with great effectiveness. He may have preached the same message repeatedly to various audiences. While he probably was not invited to visit the king, Jonah's message made such a stir in the city that it reached the king.

The people of Nineveh responded to Jonah's message and repented. God noticed the repentance of Nineveh and had mercy on the city. To Jonah's anger and frustration, Nineveh did not suffer judgment at that time.

Jonah witnessed the power of the Word of God to save a city. God's Word through Jonah caused a citywide repentance. They also changed their actions by turning from their sins, specifically violence. The city was about to be destroyed, but because of their response to Jonah's message the city was saved.

A Transforming City is Repentant

I was visiting the Charlottesville, VA, area when the KKK held a tiny rally. A handful of Klansmen were met by thousands of counter protestors. In the post-rally discussions one person commented that she did not support either the KKK or the counter protestors. I do not know anything about the person who made this comment, but it is a safe bet that they are white and middle class. Only someone who is white and has money can avoid the issue of a group that hates people of color coming to town. The comment exposes the dangers of ultra-individualism. The people of faith cannot watch others suffer injustice and not get involved. We need to break away from an overly individualistic approach to faith that does not leave room for public sins.

When social sins are ignored, they are allowed to continue unimpeded. Even if social sins are not the specific sin of an individual person, they still need to be mourned over and repented of by the people of God. The important point is that we need to care about other people's problems. We need to think communally; if one part of our community suffers, we all suffer.

The prophetic announcement of the impending destruction of Nineveh resulted in public mourning. Wearing sackcloth, sitting in ashes, and fasting are all associated with mourning. This was a citywide lament by decree of the king with the objective of saving the city from God's destruction.

Nineveh was a power center of the region's superpower. For all practical purposes, it was the Evil Empire. The Assyrian war machine was immense. Their whole way of life revolved around war. Wherever the Assyrian armies went, piles of dead bodies followed. The level of Assyrian's violence is on par with the most horrific war crimes today. Bakke describes the viciousness of the Assyrian army.

> The Assyrians were the Nazis of the ancient world. They were the most violent culture in the Middle East. The Assyrian army would raid a village, put out the eyes of the oldest men and murder the women and children in front of them, so the blinded victims could hear the death cries of their families. After stacking the bodies in the street like cordwood, the army would move to the next village.[45]

The people of Nineveh certainly had a lot of reasons to repent. The city that spread fear and death in its wake has done a 180. They are now expressing remorse over their actions.

Nineveh's repentance moved God to not destroy the city at that time. Yet, it did not last. Assyria as a nation still practiced military domination. They still killed, exploited, and oppressed the nations within their reach. Jonah's prophesy of destruction eventually came in 612 BC when Babylon captured Nineveh.

The expression of lament must be genuine. It cannot be manipulated into a law or church program. When the king made the decree that everyone was to mourn, he simply put to law what was already happening. It was the common citizens of Nineveh that heard Jonah's preaching and responded with mourning.

Nineveh experienced citywide repentance with everyone from common citizens to the king engaging in ceremonial mourning and turning from their sins. The king went so far as to issue a citywide fast for both people and livestock. There was an official call to seek God in prayer. The mourning was followed by a change of action. "Let everyone turn from his evil way and from the violence that is in his hands" (Jonah 3:8). The specific focus of this repentance was their violence. The king knew their guilt and sought change.

Remorse is the first step of repentance. Repentance cannot happen unless there is sadness over past actions. When our actions are viewed from the perspective of those who suffer the consequences of them, we are freed to mourn. It is through mourning that we are moved to repent.

Jesus mentioned the repentance of the people of Nineveh to challenge the crowd to repent (Luke 11:32). If the Ninevites repented when they heard Jonah preach, Jesus' generation should have repented when they heard Jesus.

Transformation cannot ignore historical sins. There are sins in the past that still impact the social climate of some communities. Historical racism and oppressive policies have impoverished many urban neighborhoods. The saying, "white man's roads through black man's homes" is not merely a slogan, but an actual description of the reality of most American cities. The convenience of rich and middle-class suburban whites to drive on high-speed highways causes the suffering of low-income African Americans. Churches need to take steps of public repentance for their sins. Many have already done this and are encouraged to continue to work for healing and restoration as a way to move forward for a more just city.

I witnessed a powerful repentance of historical sins when a prominent Japanese biblical scholar spoke during a chapel service at Asian Theological Seminary in Manila, Philippines. The message focused on the sins of Japanese soldiers during World War II. He explained the horrors that many Filipina women faced when they were forced into sexual slavery. After mourning over the sins of his people he then asked the predominately Filipino audience for forgiveness.

Of course, current sins must also be confessed. There are also current sins that hold community residents enslaved in its grip. Freedom begins with repenting of the dominant community sins.

Repentance is more than a prayer asking for God's forgiveness. It is calling on God for the strength to turn from social sins. There must be a change of thinking and behavior that goes along with repentance.

Reflection and Action

1. How should churches go about publicly confessing historical injustices?
2. How can your church create a culture of repentance and restoration?
3. Spend time mourning over one of the injustices in your area and lift it up to God in a prayer of confession.

Chapter 28

Transformation Starts as a Trickle: Reflections on Ezekiel 47:1-12

Then he brought me back to the door of the temple, and behold, water was issuing from below the threshold of the temple toward the east (for the temple faced east). The water was flowing down from below the south end of the threshold of the temple, south of the altar. Then he brought me out by way of the north gate and led me around on the outside to the outer gate that faces toward the east; and behold, the water was trickling out on the south side. Going on eastward with a measuring line in his hand, the man measured a thousand cubits, and then led me through the water, and it was ankle-deep. Again he measured a thousand, and led me through the water, and it was knee-deep. Again he measured a thousand, and led me through the water, and it was waist-deep. Again he measured a thousand, and it was a river that I could not pass through, for the water had risen. It was deep enough to swim in, a river that could not be passed through. And he said to me, "Son of man, have you seen this?" Then he led me back to the bank of the river. As I went back, I saw on the bank of the river very many trees on the one side and on the other. And he said to me,

"This water flows toward the eastern region and goes down into the Arabah, and enters the sea; when the water flows into the sea, the water will become fresh. And wherever the river goes, every living creature that swarms will live, and there will be very many fish. For this water goes there, that the waters of the sea may become fresh; so everything will live where the river goes. Fishermen will stand beside the sea. From Engedi to Eneglaim it will be a place for the spreading of nets. Its fish will be of very many kinds, like the fish of the Great Sea. But its swamps and marshes will not become fresh; they are to be left for salt. And on the banks, on both sides of the river, there will grow all kinds of trees for food. Their leaves will not wither, nor their fruit fail, but they will bear fresh fruit every month, because the water for them flows from the sanctuary. Their fruit will be for food, and their leaves for healing" (Ezekiel 47:1-12).

Ezekiel's vision of the transformed city (Ezek. 40-48) included the symbolic living water flowing from the temple. Jerusalem does not have an actual river flowing from it, but it does have springs. The source of the river is the presence of God. The river in Ezekiel's vision has extraordinary life-giving power. The trees are able to produce fruit on a monthly basis. This miraculous river is meant to be symbolic of the effect of God's glory returning to the temple.

A Trickle from the Temple becomes the River of Life

The water flowing from the temple started as a trickle. The angel takes Ezekiel further and further from the temple and the drops of water eventually form a huge river. It started out small but ended up having a huge impact on the city and beyond. After the river healed the land, the boundaries were divided up according to the tribes of Israel.

Ezekiel's vision of the river would have encouraged the exiles since it symbolized the end of God's judgment upon the nation and the land. God's favor would once again be upon his people. God has returned to dwell in his beloved city and is bringing life and healing to the land. God's presence is the source of all life.

There is a future hope since Ezekiel's vision will not be entirely fulfilled with the rebuilding of Jerusalem and the temple. A time will eventually come when God's reign will be in its full glory. God's people will live in his presence enjoying the abundance of his provisions.

Rivers have importance throughout Scripture. The four great rivers of the Garden of Eden, the Nile in Egypt, and the Jordan are just a few of the rivers in Scripture. In dry climates, rivers are the source of life-giving water. Rivers provide the vital lifeline for crop production allowing the land to support growing cities.

Jesus picked up on the living water metaphor to describe himself (John 4:10-15). Jesus used this fact of nature to teach that he is the one who truly sustains all life. Jesus is the water of life. Jesus' water is eternally satisfying. He told the Samaritan woman at the well, "Whoever drinks of the water that I will give him will never be thirsty again. The water that I will give him will become in him a spring of water welling up to eternal life" (John 4:14).

The New Jerusalem has a river of life (Rev. 22:1-2). Without a temple in the New Jerusalem the river of life flows from the throne of God. The river flows through the streets of the city and the tree of life is on both sides of the river. The tree of life yields a different fruit each month and its leaves are for the healing of the nations (Rev. 22:1-5).

Transformation Starts Small

Both the downfall and restoration of Jerusalem took years. The cities of Judah lay in ruins for many generations. War had initially destroyed the cities and the land, but it was years of neglect that kept them in a state of disrepair.

Likewise, transformation does not happen in a day. It is a long, slow process that takes generations. The rebuilders are the local residents working over many generations. The collective effort decade after decade is the ongoing process of transformation. It is a trickle of living water that slowly improves the area within its circle of influence.

Knowing that transformation starts small and is generational allows for realistic expectations. Expecting someone to go from homeless and unemployed to earning enough to pay for rent and food within one year is just not realistic for most people. For many it takes years to get off the streets and into housing. Simply going to school to get credentials or degrees can take years, especially if it is part-time while also working.

A long-term understanding of transformation is needed to develop leaders that will continue to serve their community into the future. Perkins writes, "It takes time to develop and grow what our urban communities need most: indigenous leaders. Quick-fix solutions cannot truly develop people."[46] Trash can be removed from a vacant lot in a day, but in order to keep it clean we must invest long-term in the development of local leaders.

There are going to be ups and downs in the day-to-day work. The work can sometimes seem painfully slow. It is often two steps forward and one step backward. It can sometimes feel like running on a treadmill, working hard but not getting anywhere. A long-term vision for transformation helps to keep us hopeful by focusing on God and not being discouraged by the current situation.

There is never really a finish line in community work. Projects can be finished, but transformation is an ongoing process. It is a journey. God is in control of transformation, through all the starts and stops along the way.

The church planting movement of the early church as recorded in Acts started small and spread from city to city. Paul and his mission team went from city to city planting churches and leaving capable leaders to continue the work. From Jerusalem to Rome, cities of the ancient Near East were impacted and transformed by the mission of the early church.

The work almost always starts small. When the mission team first moved into the railroad community of Balic-Balic they did not know the impact their obscure work would have. Balic-Balic Christian Church (BBCC) started as a small church and stayed small throughout its entire existence until the government demolished the church and community. The discipleship process was painfully slow. It is impossible to count the number of times the church workers wanted to give up on some of the members thinking the discipleship process was going nowhere. It is only in hindsight that the fruit of the small church plant can be seen.

Before the demolition, the small church started reaching out to other railroad communities. They began home Bible studies and a house church in an area along the tracks that also included land beyond the boundary of the demolition. The area past the train property was not demolished. By the providence of God, the exact place that would not be affected by the demolition was where the work started and continues to this day. After the demolition the church members scattered and have gotten involved in churches and ministries in the various communities throughout the city. They are having an impact beyond the neighborhood where the church was located.

Reflection and Action

1. What has started out small but ended up having a large impact in your city?

2. What small steps can you take in the work of transformation in your community?

Chapter 29

Transformation is Interconnected: Reflections on Isaiah 61:1-4

> The Spirit of the Lord GOD is upon me, because the LORD has anointed me to bring good news to the poor; he has sent me to bind up the brokenhearted, to proclaim liberty to the captives, and the opening of the prison to those who are bound; to proclaim the year of the LORD's favor, and the day of vengeance of our God; to comfort all who mourn; to grant to those who mourn in Zion—to give them a beautiful headdress instead of ashes, the oil of gladness instead of mourning, the garment of praise instead of a faint spirit; that they may be called oaks of righteousness, the planting of the LORD, that he may be glorified. They shall build up the ancient ruins; they shall raise up the former devastations; they shall repair the ruined cities, the devastations of many generations (Isaiah 61:1-4).

Work in a specific community has to be viewed as interconnected with other communities, towns, cities, and nations. Communities, cities, and nations do not exist in isolation. We live in a globalized world. A hurricane in Texas raises the price of gas around the world.

Isaiah proclaimed, "the year of the LORD's favor" (Isa. 61:2). The year of the Lord's favor is a reference to the Year of Jubilee. This was a time of letting the land rest, canceling debts, freeing slaves, and returning farmland to its original owners (Lev. 25:8-34). The Year of Jubilee was to prevent excessive wealth and poverty from being passed down from generation to generation. Part of the good news to be preached to the poor was the announcement of the Year of Jubilee.

The poor, brokenhearted, captives, and prisoners were to symbolically put on a beautiful headdress, oil of gladness, and a garment of praise. They are undergoing transformation and it shows. The poor in the ruins of Judah's cities were singled out as the ones who would hear the good news. The time of sadness has ended.

They were now planted by God to be oaks of righteousness for his glory. Oaks are sturdy hardwood trees that are both large and strong. Likewise, the righteousness of the people of God was to be large and strong.

God would be glorified through the emotional and spiritual transformation of the people. Instead of mourning there would be joy. Instead of robbery and wrong there would be righteousness. Not a flimsy righteousness when it is convenient, but one that stands strong in God.

The situation of the land at that time was ruined cities. War and neglect had destroyed the land and its cities. The natural result of the emotional and spiritual transformation for the glory of God is rebuilding their cities.

The rebuilders of the city are the poor, brokenhearted, captives, and prisoners. Isaiah's preaching in the power of the Spirit encouraged the poor to work for their liberation. The role of the church is not to provide programs for the poor but to join them in their work to improve their lives.

Jesus in the Synagogue at Nazareth

Isaiah's words were good news to the returning exiles even though the complete fulfillment was in Jesus (Luke 4:16-18). When Jesus delivered his sermon in the synagogue at Nazareth, he read from Isaiah 61:1-2, inserting Isaiah 58:6. Both passages refer to the Year of Jubilee and touch on urban transformation. Jesus is the fulfillment of Isaiah's words.

Jesus' application of Isaiah 61 was the announcement of the focus of his ministry. His ministry was one of proclaiming good news to the poor and healing the sick and demon possessed. Jesus used a passage on rebuilding cities to introduce his preaching and healing ministry.

Transformation is Interconnected

Ancient ruins will be built up, and ruined cities will be repaired. Both ruins and cities are plural. The rebuilding was not limited to one community or city. Jerusalem was the capital city and the place chosen by God where his temple was to be rebuilt. It was an important city for the people of God. Yet, Jerusalem was just one of many cities destroyed during the Babylonian conquest. Therefore the rebuilding had to extend beyond Jerusalem for the nation to be rebuilt.

Other prophets also recognized that the process of rebuilding was not limited to one city or region. Jeremiah wrote,

> Thus says the LORD of hosts: In this place that is waste, without man or beast, and in all of its cities, there shall again be habitations of shepherds resting their flocks. In the cities of the hill country, in the cities of the Shephelah, and in the cities of the Negeb, in the land of Benjamin, the places about Jerusalem, and in the cities of Judah, flocks shall again pass under the hands of the one who counts them, says the LORD (Jer. 33:12-13).

The vision of urban transformation presented by Amos was nationwide. "I will restore the fortunes of my people Israel, and they shall rebuild the ruined cities and inhabit them" (Amos 9:14). This is not simply the rebuilding of Samaria, Israel's capital city. It was the rebuilding of ruined cities throughout the nation.

Jerusalem was not rebuilt at the expense of the rest of the country. It is possible to build a city or community while destroying another in the process. When a large business decides to close its doors in one location and reopen somewhere else, one location's gain is another's loss. Infrastructure such as the exact location of major roads, bridges, and train stations can lead to the decay or flourishing of neighborhoods. Development projects must always ask who is being hurt in the process.

Transformation has to look beyond individual communities and cities. Pouring money into developing a city's business district while low-income communities are neglected is unacceptable. Policies of concentrating poverty, drugs, and violence in certain areas are oppressive.

Reducing homelessness in a particular city can be deceptive. Many cities' "solution" to homelessness is to make life as difficult as possible for the homeless so they move somewhere else. Merely shifting the homeless to other locations is not a solution.

The interconnectedness of communities needs to influence planning and evaluation of engagement. As we work locally, we must continually look elsewhere so that others are not left behind. It is important to know how engagement impacts the marginalized in other communities and beyond.

An interconnected perspective of transformation helps us to work for win-win solutions. Striving for win-win is to ensure that there are no losers. It's not wealthy subdivisions against low-income communities, or light rail versus bike lanes. Transformation must seek a win-win solution for all stakeholders.

Win-win does not mean that everyone will equally benefit. Some may even face short-term loses in the transition period, particularly the wealthy who benefit from the status quo. It may take time for some to adjust to the changes. But in the long-term, win-win is possible.

Reflection and Action

1. Describe an example from your city of one area benefitting at the expense of another.

2. How can your community engagement be mindful of its impact on other areas?

Chapter 30

A Reconciled Community Gathering in the Presence of the Lord: Reflections on Jeremiah 3:14-18

> Return, O faithless children, declares the LORD; for I am your master; I will take you, one from a city and two from a family, and I will bring you to Zion. And I will give you shepherds after my own heart, who will feed you with knowledge and understanding. And when you have multiplied and been fruitful in the land, in those days, declares the LORD, they shall no more say, "The ark of the covenant of the LORD." It shall not come to mind or be remembered or missed; it shall not be made again. At that time Jerusalem shall be called the throne of the LORD, and all nations shall gather to it, to the presence of the LORD in Jerusalem, and they shall no more stubbornly follow their own evil heart. In those days the house of Judah shall join the house of Israel, and together they shall come from the land of the north to the land that I gave your fathers for a heritage (Jeremiah 3:14-18).

It is beautiful to see the people of God gathering together to worship across class and ethnic barriers. I was invited to a home Bible study in San Antonio, TX and quickly observed the reconciling power of the gospel. The homeowner was an older African American woman. Her housemates included a middle-aged white woman, a paralyzed Mexican man, and a young white woman. I was intrigued by the diversity of the household so I inquired about how it came about. This reconciled community was the result of reaching out in love to others in need. The middle-aged white woman took care of the paralyzed Mexican man after he was shot during a robbery. The African American homeowner invited the two of them to live with her because her home was already wheelchair accessible. The young white woman was about to become homeless, so she was also invited to move in. The four of them now live, worship, and study the Bible together as a testimony to the reconciling power of the gospel. This is living out the commandment to love your neighbor as yourself.

Jeremiah's message of hope begins with the call to repent. The people were to return to the Lord even though it would be small, one from a city and two from a family. Ones and twos are not a mass of people. It is the small and faithful remnant that God brings together to work for reconciliation and transformation.

The Ark of the Covenant will not come to mind. The Ark of the Covenant symbolized the presence of God (see Exod. 25:22; Lev. 16:2; 1 Sam. 4:4). The city itself will become the symbol of God's presence because it is where God dwells. The city will be called "the throne of the LORD" (Jer. 3:17), the place where God sits. There will be the knowledge and understanding that God is in their midst so the use of special symbols to remind them of God's presence will be unnecessary.

Jerusalem will be the place where the nations gather to worship. The people will be freed from the slavery of their evil hearts, and Israel and Judah will be united. The reconciliation between Israel and Judah points to the power of God to the nations that have gathered to worship in Jerusalem.

The restoration of the city is extensive and all-inclusive. The message of hope was for the full restoration of the city. This was well beyond what they could have even hoped for when the city sat in ruins.

The work that God is doing will bring reconciliation between Judah and Israel. By the time of the exile, Israel and Judah had been divided for centuries. Although they viewed each other as cousins, they still fought wars against each other. In the restored city the power of God replaces old animosities with forgiveness. Reconciliation and forgiveness bring people together in worship.

Gathering together to worship is rooted in loving God and loving neighbors. The exiles needed to replace oppression and exploitation with righteousness and justice. The reconciliation was not a superficial pleasantness when they were around each other. They were a truly transformed and reconciled community.

Reconciliation is an important part of transformation. Racial reconciliation is an on-going work of the church. Perkins writes, "His Word made it clear that racial reconciliation was not only possible, but mandatory for the Body of Christ."[47] Working for racial reconciliation is one aspect of what it means to love our neighbors as ourselves. Therefore, it must be prioritized.

Reconciliation must unite groups divided by society. A lesser-discussed need is the reconciliation between social classes. In the US, cross-class reconciliation is very challenging because of class-based segregation. People are divided by class through zoning laws that ensure people of similar income levels all live in the same neighborhood.

Cross-class reconciliation can result in awkward situations. A wealthy businessman gave free tickets for our church to watch a stage play. The play was held in an upscale theater. The lobby was carpeted and had a huge chandelier. While standing in the lobby the guys from our church decided to find out what it was like to lie on a carpet. To my embarrassment, they each took turns lying down on the carpet. After attracting lots of attention to ourselves we finally found our seats. Soon after the play started, I looked over to see how they were doing. Every one of them was asleep.

A transforming community is one in which people are gathering together to worship. This gathering is not in homogeneous churches where people from the same ethnicity and social class come together. The gathering together of the people of God from all walks of life is one form of reconciliation.

Churches need to become intentional about representing community demographics. The natural tendency is to become homogeneous. In order to faithfully proclaim the reconciling power of the cross, the church must seek to become a reconciled cross-class, multiethnic community.

The first area of reconciliation needed is within families. My friend Chris had the privilege of being used by Jesus to help the reconciliation of adult siblings who have not talked in over a decade. Chris' neighbor Jeremy is mentally ill, and very reserved. Chris was eventually able to help Jeremy get treatment and medication for his psychological condition. With medication and healthy human interaction Jeremy's condition improved.

As their friendship developed, Jeremy finally revealed that he has a sister. They have been estranged for more than ten years because of the abusive way he treated her due to his mental illness. Jeremy's health is deteriorating so he wanted to be reconciled with her before it's too late.

Chris was able to locate Jeremy's sister. They met in person and he gave her an update on how Jeremy was doing. She agreed to meet with Jeremy on the condition that Chris would also be there. When Chris told Jeremy that his sister was willing to come see him again after so many years he was overcome with joy.

Chris told Jeremy that God was giving him a chance to be reconciled to his sister, and he had to be kind and respectful. Jeremy tried to minimize his previous behavior by saying it wasn't that frequent. Chris challenged him not to downplay what he had done, but to actually apologize to his sister by telling her, "I am sorry for how I treated you."

Jeremy sometimes referred to himself as "the Lord's man" when he talks about some of the odd things that he thinks God tells him to do. In response to this Chris said, "Jeremy, you are the Lord's man. You have to do what Jesus would do in this situation. Jesus breaks down the dividing walls of hostility and reconciles us to God and to one another. Jesus teaches us to leave a gift behind at God's altar in order to first be reconciled with a sister or brother. You are the Lord's man. You need to take the first step and apologize to your sister for how you treated her. Show her kindness and respect from now on, and be reconciled to her. Do you think you can do that?"

The next day his sister came, and he did it. He apologized to her and spoke respectfully. Their relationship was restored, and they embraced. They began spending time together, and she started taking responsibility for the things that Jeremy can no longer do for himself. She also began looking into options for his care going forward. It is beautiful to see this family reunited after so many years.

God's timing in the reconciliation was perfect. Jeremy owns his home, but due to his mental illness he did not stay on top of paying his property taxes. When his sister re-entered his life, she discovered that he owed thousands of dollars in back property taxes. She also discovered that his house was due to go up for auction that month. By God's grace, the city was missing one document they needed to move forward, so the auction was postponed. Jeremy's sister took out a loan to pay off the property tax bill, so he would not lose his home. If Jeremy had not reconnected and reconciled with his sister when he did, his house almost certainly would have been sold out from under him, and he would be homeless today.

Reflection and Action

1. What groups are in need of reconciliation in your community?
2. Set a meeting with a leader from a church different from yours to discuss reconciliation in your community.

Chapter 31

Removing Those Who Are Destructive to The Neighborhood

Reflections on Zephaniah 3:14-20

Sing aloud, O daughter of Zion; shout, O Israel! Rejoice and exult with all your heart, O daughter of Jerusalem! The LORD has taken away the judgments against you; he has cleared away your enemies. The King of Israel, the LORD, is in your midst; you shall never again fear evil. On that day it shall be said to Jerusalem: "Fear not, O Zion; let not your hands grow weak. The LORD your God is in your midst, a mighty one who will save; he will rejoice over you with gladness; he will quiet you by his love; he will exult over you with loud singing. I will gather those of you who mourn for the festival, so that you will no longer suffer reproach. Behold, at that time I will deal with all your oppressors. And I will save the lame and gather the outcast, and I will change their shame into praise and renown in all the earth. At that time I will bring you in, at the time when I gather you together; for I will make you renowned and praised among all the peoples of the earth, when I restore your fortunes before your eyes," says the LORD (Zephaniah 3:14-20).

Zephaniah prophesied in Judah during Josiah's reign and was a contemporary of Jeremiah. The long rebellious reign of Josiah's grandfather Manasseh had turned the people away from God. There was rampant idolatry, greed, violence, and deceit (Zep. 1). Zephaniah's message was mostly that of judgment for both Judah's enemies as well as for Jerusalem itself. Zephaniah gave Jerusalem a strong warning of God's judgment. "Woe to her who is rebellious and defiled, the oppressing city!" (Zep. 3:1). It did not take long for Zephaniah's prophecy to be fulfilled. Babylon destroyed Jerusalem just over twenty years after Josiah died. Yet there is still a glimmer of hope as the book of Zephaniah ends with restoration.

Zephaniah calls for joy and celebration because the judgment is over and the enemy has been removed. The residents were to shout for joy and exult with their heart (Zep. 3:14). This was to be a time of celebration because God was in their midst (Zep. 3:15). The city does not have to live in fear since God is its protector. God will gather the exiles and bring them back to Jerusalem. He will also restore the fortunes of the city.

God celebrates his work of restoring the city. He rejoices over the city and will exalt the city with singing. This seems backward. The city should rejoice in God, which it does, but it can also make God glad. The city's transformation is all God's doing. It is right for God to be glad in his work.

God assured the people that he would deal with their oppressors. The restoration of the people of God was accompanied by judgment upon oppressors. Part of how God deals with oppressors is to remove them from the position of being able to oppress.

Removing Harmful People from a Community

Caleb was an alcoholic, addicted to drugs, and highly unpredictable. He would often yell threats at random people walking past him. He was also in the habit of stalking women by following them and even sleeping outside their houses. Caleb began to follow my wife around. If she walked past him, he would swing his arm out toward her, trying to touch her inappropriately. I had to accompany her whenever she left the house. We prayed that Caleb would either become a Christian or that God would remove him from the community. The following Sunday, he came to church but walked out before the service was over. A few months later, he was arrested for breaking and entering but was released shortly after his arrest, and he showed no signs of change. He was also arrested for following a high school girl all the way to her school and trying to enter her classroom. Soon after that his younger brother told me that Caleb had stabbed another man to death and had been arrested for homicide. This meant that he was permanently removed from the community.

With Caleb gone there was a noticeable change in the community. Women were no longer concerned about sexual harassment every time they went outside. The random yelling and threats ceased. The community became a more pleasant place to live.

My interaction with Caleb did not end with his arrest. I could have said good riddance and been done with him. But God had different plans. At that time, I was going with a group of men from my church to help with a prison Bible study. It turned out that Caleb was in the same section of the jail where we led the Bible study. In jail, he was sober, and I was able to have actual conversations with him. He turned out to be our prison evangelist who would round up men to join our Bible study.

Removing harmful people from a community can help it to be a more peaceful place to live. One of the reasons why Zephaniah declared a celebration was that God had cleared away their enemies. Psalm 101 is a political Psalm of justice. David reflects on his role as king. "Morning by morning I will destroy all the wicked in the land, cutting off all the evildoers from the city of the LORD" (Ps. 101:8). The removal of evildoers from the city is one part of spiritual renewal. It is a reality that some people are detrimental to community life. Engagement for transformation will sometimes involve the removal of harmful people and businesses. This may sound harsh, but anyone who has lived on a block with a drug house, or watched a business suck the hope out of residents, knows that their removal can change a community.

Isaiah used the imagery of purifying metal to describe how God removed Israel's leaders (Isa. 1:25). God was going to clean house and get rid of oppressive and corrupt rulers. The destructive elements within society will be removed. In Isaiah's case, the city's leaders had turned from God and become corrupt. They pulled the whole nation away from God.

Removing harmful people is not about revenge or demonizing others. After a fire destroyed a large section of my community, some of those who lost everything wrote a petition and collected signatures to have the woman who started the fire kicked out of our neighborhood. The fire may have been caused by her carelessness, but it certainly was not intentional. She too lost her home and all of her belongings. The desire to have her removed was about revenge, not making the community a safer place to live.

We should never demonize anyone regardless of how evil we think they are. Everyone can change. A person involved in a racist organization can become friends with someone of another ethnicity and renounce their past hatred. Oppressive business owners can repent of their actions and operate their businesses from a justice perspective.

God can change anyone and ideally the problem people in the community turn to Christ and allow God to transform their lives. In my church there are many people who were once harmful to the community but now contribute to neighborhood life. Yet, there are still people in my community that sell drugs and cause problems. As much as we would like to see problem people come to know Jesus, the reality is that not everyone will. Some people will continue to harm their communities.

Removing drug dealers is not easy or safe. Pastors and other workers have received death threats and slanderous accusations. A drug dealer told one pastor that I know he was welcome to teach the Bible, but if he tried to stop the sale of drugs, "bad things would happen to him."

Removing harmful people from a community needs to be done in humility, prayer, and love for the person being removed. It is not about moving problem people to another community for them to become someone else's problem. Some people improve once they are in a new location. I led a Bible study with a small-time drug dealer who desperately wanted out, but could not as long as he remained in his neighborhood. He even told me that he wanted to move so he could get away from his friends that pressured him to sell drugs. Eventually, he did move and he was able to finally stop selling drugs for good. His removal from his old neighborhood was a win-win for both himself and the community.

In some cases, it is not individuals that are harmful to a community, but businesses. A neighborhood organization in Los Angeles worked to close down a liquor store that served as a cover for a local gang in their drug dealing and prostitution. The owner was Asian and accused the neighborhood organization of wanting to close the store because they were racist against Asians. He was even able to get a civil rights lawyer to take his case free of charge. The neighborhood organization was able to prevail but only after a long, painful fight. The liquor store was sold and is now a small grocery store. The gang, drug, and prostitution activity in that area greatly diminished after the liquor store closed.

Reflection and Action

1. How do you determine who is truly harmful to your community as opposed to someone you simply do not get along with and would prefer they move?
2. What types of businesses are potentially harmful for your community?

Chapter 32

Peace and Transformation: Reflections on Isaiah 2:1-5

The word that Isaiah the son of Amoz saw concerning Judah and Jerusalem. It shall come to pass in the latter days that the mountain of the house of the LORD shall be established as the highest of the mountains, and shall be lifted up above the hills; and all the nations shall flow to it, and many peoples shall come, and say: "Come, let us go up to the mountain of the LORD, to the house of the God of Jacob, that he may teach us his ways and that we may walk in his paths." For out of Zion shall go the law, and the word of the LORD from Jerusalem. He shall judge between the nations, and shall decide disputes for many peoples; and they shall beat their swords into plowshares, and their spears into pruning hooks; nation shall not lift up sword against nation, neither shall they learn war anymore. O house of Jacob, come, let us walk in the light of the LORD (Isaiah 2:1-5).

Isaiah saw a glorious vision concerning the restoration of Jerusalem and he wanted the people to respond appropriately. They were to walk in God's paths. Walking in the path of God is to be in a relationship with him and living in obedience to his Word. To walk in God's path is to reject the culture of greed and violence and embrace the God of love. It is to obey the greatest commandment of loving God and loving others (Matt. 22:36-40). A transforming city walks in the path of God to find peace.

Both the restored Jerusalem and the Jerusalem during the time of Isaiah were multinational and multiethnic. The difference is that the restored Jerusalem was a multinational, multiethnic community joined together in the worship of the one true God. The Jerusalem of Isaiah's day was a multinational, multiethnic city that worshiped many gods and was syncretistic in its beliefs.

Revising Violence-Inciting Laws

No modern political nation represents the people of God and therefore their laws cannot be equated with God's law. The kingdom of God is not a political state. Humans write the laws that govern the land. Even laws with the best intentions can be corrupted by sin. One part of the transformation process includes a thorough revision of a city's laws to ensure that the legal system is not oppressive. Simple questions such as, "Who does this law benefit?" and "Who does this law hurt?" can be used to guide the evaluation process.

Unjust laws result in policies designed to expand the bottom line of the already rich regardless of their impact on everyone else. Unjust laws that oppress the poor eventually lead to social unrest and sometimes violence as the marginalized struggle for liberation. The violence more often than not comes from those wanting to maintain the oppressive status quo.

It is not just the poor who suffer because of inequality. Professors Richard Wilkinson and Kate Pickett write, "The vast majority of the population is harmed by greater inequality."[48] This can be addressed by revising violence-inducing laws.

Engagement for transformation must address the issue of legalized oppression. Efforts by the poor to improve their lives should not be swept away by injustice (Pr. 13:23). The legal structure must prevent the concentration of wealth in the hands of a few elite.

A Transforming Community is a Place of Peace

I was hanging out at a basketball court near my house when I observed a group of pre-teen boys showing each other their homemade brass knuckles. The most talkative of the group started telling a story about getting into a fight. As he dramatized the story, he put on the brass knuckles and punched the air saying he knocked the other kid backwards. He then explained that he kicked him while he was down and finished him off with another blow from the brass knuckles. I am sure the story was exaggerated if not entirely made up, but he still impressed all of his friends.

Eventually, they ended up right next to me so I asked if I could see the brass knuckles. As I held them, he explained what they were made of. I told him not to punch anyone with them so he replied, "they just cause a little bit of blood." I warned him that he might end up having to pay expensive hospital bills if he injured another kid with them.

The whole interaction saddened me as it exposed the lust for violence present in today's culture. The boys were respectful and would hopefully not act out their violent fantasies. Sadly, fights are fairly common, so they have lots of opportunities to get their adrenaline rush by getting into a fight.

In some communities where kids carry guns and are killing each other, brass knuckles would be a welcomed improvement, albeit certainly not the end goal. The boys taking apart their brass knuckles and turning them into game pieces would be a beautiful example of overcoming the craving for violence.

A transforming community is a place of peace through having the integrity to speak for peace and the courage to negotiate peace. In violent plagued communities the dream of peace is difficult to even hope for. The railroad community of Balic-Balic, Manila, Philippines, was all too familiar with violence. The numerous drug houses in the area meant the neighborhood was a hotbed for violence. The police only added to the danger by their own violent tactics. Yet, with all the shootouts and killings there was one small section of the tracks that was noticeably different. Balic-Balic Christian Church (BBCC) met in a rented house in this notorious community. Many of the members lived in the immediate vicinity of the church. Instead of using guns to combat drug houses, they reached out in love with the transforming power of Jesus. The Word of God was studied in homes, and people came to faith in Jesus. God was working in mighty ways to create a small area of peace in the midst of violence.

Isaiah's vision of a transformed city was not one of military might. The Israelites were not commanded to have the largest army with the most sophisticated weapons. The city was to be transformed for God's glory, not as a tool of domination.

The result of the increasing influence of laws of justice and walking in the path of God will be peace. Isaiah described military weapons being turned into farm tools. Tools of death and destruction were being transformed into tools that help provide life-giving food. Weapons were removed and the knowledge of war decreased as people no longer trained to fight.

Isaiah was referring to peace on a national scale. He looked to a time when war between nations ceases. Biblical scholar Joseph Blenkinsopp writes, "In view of our own sad and guilty knowledge of the violence we continue to visit on each other, on other creatures, and on the environment in general, the eschatological horizon of the abolition of war, and even of violence in the animal world (11:6-9), is one of the most poignant motifs in the book."[49] Isaiah's message is a call for demilitarization.

Isaiah speaks of two ways that peace is achieved. The first is to take away the availability of weapons and the second is to limit the knowledge of how to wage war. Both approaches are important components of helping a nation become a place of peace.

At the community level, taking weapons off the streets is a basic way to try to make a city more peaceful. This should start with the demilitarization of the police force. Military surplus equipment and weapons should never be given to police departments and what they were given must be returned. It is very dangerous when governments give police the capacity and legal authority to kill citizens.

The issue of limiting the availability of weapons on the streets is cultural. As long as the culture is addicted to violence there will be weapons available to commit violence. Peacemakers are needed to change the culture of violence and limit the desire for weapons.

Limiting the knowledge of how to fight on the street level is having positive alternatives to violence. Schools need to invest in extracurricular activities such as clubs and sports. Athletic programs can have a positive impact in the lives of students. Involvement in school sports kept me from spending my time in unhealthy activities that could have led to violence. Fighting was out of the question because it would have resulted in suspension and possibly being kicked off the team.

There is an important difference between forgetting how to wage war and forgetting the horrors of war. Both are the natural result of prolonged peace. Yet the outcome can be vastly different. Forgetting how to wage war continues the time of peace while forgetting the horrors of war can lead to the desire for war. The horrors of war must never be forgotten. Within a neighborhood setting, the horrors of street violence should also never be forgotten.

There will be peace in the city. "Violence shall no longer be heard in the land" (Isa. 60:18). Jerusalem was plagued by violence. The cycle of violence was magnified by the city's current condition of lacking a defensive wall. The physical destruction of the city, and its spiritual darkness meant that it was a breeding ground for violence.

Peace means that people can hang out in a neighborhood without fear. Children can play in parks and seniors can go for walks without worrying about what might happen. Peace also means that police officers serve and protect the neighborhood, not harass and intimidate the residents while dressed like soldiers.

Peace is dependent upon factors such as hope that the community will improve and economic opportunities. When youth and young adults know that meaningful employment is within their range of options, they will take steps to fulfill those hopes. Economic opportunities also limit the need to turn to crime to survive, which contributes to peace.

Reflection and Action

1. What are some unjust and oppressive laws in your city?
2. How can you or your church be peacemakers in your city or community?

Chapter 33

Networking for Transformation: Reflections on Haggai 2:1-9

In the seventh month, on the twenty-first day of the month, the word of the LORD came by the hand of Haggai the prophet, "Speak now to Zerubbabel the son of Shealtiel, governor of Judah, and to Joshua the son of Jehozadak, the high priest, and to all the remnant of the people, and say, 'Who is left among you who saw this house in its former glory? How do you see it now? Is it not as nothing in your eyes? Yet now be strong, O Zerubbabel, declares the LORD. Be strong, O Joshua, son of Jehozadak, the high priest. Be strong, all you people of the land, declares the LORD. Work, for I am with you, declares the LORD of hosts, according to the covenant that I made with you when you came out of Egypt. My Spirit remains in your midst. Fear not. For thus says the LORD of hosts: Yet once more, in a little while, I will shake the heavens and the earth and the sea and the dry land. And I will shake all nations, so that the treasures of all nations shall come in, and I will fill this house with glory, says the LORD of hosts. The silver is mine, and the gold is mine, declares the LORD of hosts. The latter glory of this house shall be greater than the former, says the LORD of hosts. And in this place I will give peace, declares the LORD of hosts'" (Haggai 2:1-9).

Historical Setting of Haggai

Haggai was a contemporary of Zechariah writing in the post-exilic era. His prophetic ministry was in 520 BC and focused on challenging the people to complete the rebuilding of the temple.

When Babylon fell to the Persians, the exiles returned to the land of their ancestors but were quickly discouraged. Throughout the time of the Babylonian exile, Jerusalem was in ruins. The return from exile was not a return to the city's glory days. It was literally a journey to a wasteland. It is not hard to imagine the returning exiles saying, "What a dump!" The initial wave of returned exiles started to rebuild the temple, but their efforts were short lived. Construction halted and the structure sat unfinished.

The work on the temple was sporadic at best, but the private homes of the elite were completed with no expense spared (Haggai 1:4). The leaders in Jerusalem might have even diverted funds that were supposed to go to the rebuilding of the temple to build their elaborate mansions.

United for a Common Cause

Upon returning to Jerusalem from exile, the Israelites did not finish rebuilding the temple. This exposed their deteriorated spiritual condition. It essentially showed their lack of commitment to worship God and love their neighbors. Those with resources built their own homes without regard for anyone else. The well-being of the entire community as the people of God was no longer a priority.

While building individual private homes is a small part of the overall work of rebuilding a city, it is limited because it is simply the material advancement of one household and not the entire community or city. Transformation must be for the benefit of the community as a whole and not limited to certain families. The temple was a public building that was for the entire community. The completed temple had the power to unite the struggling nation under the name of the Lord.

In light of this, the temple was given priority in Haggai's rebuilding effort. Logically, it would make sense to rebuild the city's defensive wall first. But this time the temple was where the city's rebuilding effort began. At this point in time the people needed hope, and that would only be found in God. The rebuilding of the temple needed to be prioritized because they needed a communal space to come together and worship God. The care that went into its appearance represented the worthiness of the God for whom it was built. This would give them hope that God was now for them and not against them.

God commanded Haggai to speak to Zerubbabel the governor, Joshua the high priest, and the people. He asks them three questions about the former temple. "Who is left among you who saw this house in its former glory? How do you see it now? Is it not as nothing in your eyes?" (Haggai 2:3). It is possible that some of the seniors remembered the temple before it was destroyed. However, for the vast majority of the returned exiles who had no memory of the old temple, Haggai's questions set a depressing tone. The governor, high priest, and the people were to look at the pathetic condition of the temple but not lose hope. They were to be strong and work because God was with them (Haggai 2:4).

There was a job to be done rebuilding the temple and all the stakeholders had a role to play. The scale of the project was so huge that it would take the coordinated efforts of a variety of parties. Haggai, the governor, the high priest, and the people each had a role to play in the success of the rebuilding.

Haggai had the role of encouraging everyone to continue the work of rebuilding the temple until it was finished. The governor had the political power to finance the construction. The high priest could teach the spiritual benefits of the temple. The people were the ones who shoulder the taxes needed to pay for the project, and who will provide the skilled labor needed for the construction of the temple.

Rebuilding the temple required unity. Both Chronicles have an emphasis on unity with the repeated phrase "all Israel." Chronicles portrays Israel and Judah as fellow kinsmen. Those Israelites who remained faithful to God are seen as defecting to Judah where they rejoin the community of faith (2 Chron. 30:11).

Networking for Transformation

I had the privilege of visiting a number of ministries and connecting with church leaders in Hamilton, Canada. I observed many different churches and ministries that are passionate about God and their city. Churches are working together across denominational lines to address some of the issues facing their city. The desire to work together is what's exciting about the networking in Hamilton. There is the understanding that the issues facing the city are too big for one church to handle alone, and therefore, they recognize the need to work together to make their city a better place to live.

Networking is rooted in relationships. It is through these connections that we can come together to address a common cause. For this reason, it is important to continually seek to build relationships. The alumni of Asian Theological Seminary's Transformational Urban Leadership program have a strong fellowship that continues to provide a place to network with others in similar ministries. They have meetings several times a year to pray and fellowship together. They are also able to use their relational connections to serve each other's ministries. When one person shared the desire of some of her church members to start rooftop gardens, she was immediately given the contact information of someone who teaches workshops on growing vegetables in pots. This opened the door for her church to offer practical training on urban gardening.

Networking is important for engagement for transformation. No church or mission organization can effectively engage their community alone. Bakke writes, "We will never rebuild urban neighborhoods just with preachers."[50] Experts in a variety of fields are needed to transform communities.

The work of networking needs to be prioritized. Linthicum writes, "Networking is the first task any urban pastor needs to do in his or her community. It is also perhaps the most important task. For on the strength of his or her networks will stand or fall the ministry."[51] Networking takes time and effort, but it is time well spent. Whenever our alumni fellowship meets, I have to clear my schedule for that afternoon. Sometimes there are other urgent matters that need attending to, and I am tempted not to go. It is only through valuing the relationships that I have with others in the fellowship and seeing how important networking is that I am able to prioritize these meetings.

Networking takes humility and cooperation as we work together to address the large issues of the city. The skills, talents, and relationships of participating parties are united together in synergy where their effectiveness is greater than if they all simply worked alone.

It is important to realize that networking is more than about being effective. Churches are not businesses. We do not just do techniques because they make us effective. Networking is about building relationships and being transformed in the process. Linthicum writes regarding networking, "If built upon biblical foundations, it will enable the urban church to reorder and prioritize its life and mission so that it will be able to effectively join with the poor and exploited of its city in their liberation. By so joining in common cause, the church will gain the credibility to proclaim the gospel to those who formerly despised it."[52]

I am involved in a fellowship group for anyone working among the urban poor. This is an informal group that usually gathers with the agenda of spending time with like-minded people who are facing similar struggles and challenges. The relationships forged during these informal gatherings have been life-giving and contributed to my sustainability.

I have visited all of the other churches in my area in order to meet the pastors and leaders of those churches. I have also met with local government officials, and business owners. Just as importantly I try to connect with regular citizens in my community. This has helped to build relationships with a broad range of stakeholders in my neighborhood.

Reflection and Action

1. What are the large issues in your city that need networking to address?
2. Contact three church or community leaders to schedule meetings for networking.

Chapter 34

Working with Secular Governments: Reflections on Isaiah 44:24-28

Thus says the LORD, your Redeemer, who formed you from the womb: "I am the Lord, who made all things, who alone stretched out the heavens, who spread out the earth by myself, who frustrates the signs of liars and makes fools of diviners, who turns wise men back and makes their knowledge foolish, who confirms the word of his servant and fulfills the counsel of his messengers, who says of Jerusalem, 'She shall be inhabited,' and of the cities of Judah, 'They shall be built, and I will raise up their ruins'; who says to the deep, 'Be dry; I will dry up your rivers'; who says of Cyrus, 'He is my shepherd, and he shall fulfill all my purpose'; saying of Jerusalem, 'She shall be built,' and of the temple, 'Your foundation shall be laid'" (Isaiah 44:24-28).

Isaiah 44:24-28 is directly connected to the wider context of Isaiah 43-45. Isaiah had just given a critical analysis of the foolishness of idolatry (Isa. 44:9-20). Isaiah 45 is a prophecy concerning Cyrus, the Persian king who released the exiles so they could return to Jerusalem and rebuild the city and temple (Isa. 45:13). God, in his holiness, chose Cyrus to end the exile. Cyrus was not even a nominal follower of God. He was the ungodly political leader of a powerful nation. Sometimes he used his power to kill and oppress. Other times he used his power for good. Cyrus unknowingly obeyed God when he allowed the exiles to return home and gave them resources to rebuild.

Transformation and Secular Governments

Cyrus' motives were self-serving. He sent all the different exiles back to where they came from so they would rebuild their temples and pray for him. The logic was that when you have many people praying to their different gods, someone's god is going to answer favorably.

Cyrus was similar to a man I met who had a necklace with both a cross and a crescent. When asked about it he said he was a Hindu-Muslim-Christian. He wanted to follow Hinduism, Islam, and Christianity at the same time. This man was attempting to do the impossible. There are teachings in each of these faiths that are incompatible. While relativists try to hold all religious faiths together as if they are all equally true, it goes against reason to hold two opposite teachings as true. This man who claimed to be a Christian was not living in faith in the one true God. He knows that there is a god and he wants to make sure that he follows the right one so he claims to follow all of the major religions.

God used the Universalist Cyrus to be the political force behind the rebuilding of Jerusalem and the temple. Contemporary urban transformation will not get very far without working with local governments regardless of how ignorant of God they are.

Followers of Jesus have a much broader role in civic engagement than simply voting and paying taxes. Unjust laws and corrupt politicians need to be confronted. However, as much as possible, the church should seek to work with the government in the areas where the desires of the local government and God's commands in Scripture overlap.

One key area where the tension between faith in Jesus and working with secular governments plays out is when followers of Jesus are government employees. Cedric, a friend from church, is employed by the city government to organize community projects for vulnerable groups. Cedric's role continually brings up the tension between his faith and his government job. Part of his role is to submit a project proposal based on his observations of needs. He experiences the tension of questionable financial practices within the government. His budget sometimes gets used for the projects of other officials. As long as a project can be remotely connected to serving a vulnerable group other government officials can tap into Cedric's budget. The installation of CCTV cameras for example, can be legally paid for out of the budget for community projects for vulnerable groups because they add to the safety of children.

Cedric seeks to do his job to the best of his ability. He submits the project proposals that he feels are important and tries to get them approved. The key to Cedric's ability to maintain his faith and remain in his government position is the good working relationship he has with his co-workers. They know he is a Christian and respect his beliefs. He is known to be an honest worker and is respected by his co-workers.

The church I am currently involved in works with the local government in the area of education. This relationship came about when we initiated a meeting with the elected community leaders with the agenda of simply introducing ourselves to the officials. The result of that meeting led to further discussions on how we could work together to better serve our community.

Two of our church leaders are certificated teachers for Alternative Learning System, the Philippine governments' version of the preparation course for the high school equivalency exam. Upon discovering this, the local government officials invited us to work together to offer a free preparation course for the high school equivalency exam for those in our community who were unable to finish high school.

Our church is not in an official partnership and does not support all of the policies of the local government. Nor are the members obliged to vote for or support a particular politician. The integrity of their faith is maintained as we work with the government to love our neighbors by providing individualized training for those preparing to take the high school equivalency exam.

Working with the government in this context is about relationships with specific government employees and the project, not an official partnership. It is not a blanket endorsement of everything the government does. When government projects are beneficial to the community and are in alignment with our faith in Jesus, we give our full support to the effort. But when the government fails to act justly, the church has the prophetic responsibility to call out injustices.

Reflection and Action

1. In what areas are you willing to partner with secular governments?
2. In what areas will you not partner with a secular government?
3. What might working with your local government look like?

Chapter 35

Beauty and Transformation: Reflections on Isaiah 60

Arise, shine, for your light has come, and the glory of the LORD has risen upon you. For behold, darkness shall cover the earth, and thick darkness the peoples; but the LORD will arise upon you, and his glory will be seen upon you. And nations shall come to your light, and kings to the brightness of your rising. Lift up your eyes all around, and see; they all gather together, they come to you; your sons shall come from afar, and your daughters shall be carried on the hip. Then you shall see and be radiant; your heart shall thrill and exult, because the abundance of the sea shall be turned to you, the wealth of the nations shall come to you. A multitude of camels shall cover you, the young camels of Midian and Ephah; all those from Sheba shall come. They shall bring gold and frankincense, and shall bring good news, the praises of the LORD. All the flocks of Kedar shall be gathered to you; the rams of Nebaioth shall minister to you; they shall come up with acceptance on my altar, and I will beautify my beautiful house. Who are these that fly like a cloud, and like doves to their windows? For the coastlands shall hope for me, the ships of Tarshish first, to bring your children from afar, their silver and gold with them, for the name of the LORD your God, and for the Holy One of Israel, because he has made you beautiful. Foreigners shall build up your walls, and their kings shall minister to you; for in my wrath I struck you, but in my favor I have had mercy on you. Your gates shall be open continually; day and night they shall not be shut, that people may bring to you the wealth of the nations, with their kings led in procession. For the nation and kingdom that will not serve you shall perish; those nations shall be utterly laid waste. The glory of Lebanon shall come to you, the cypress, the plane, and the pine, to beautify the place of my sanctuary, and I will make the place of my feet glorious (Isaiah 60:1-13).

The exile was over, but Jerusalem still lay in ruins. The situation was both physically and spiritually bleak. The mounds of rubble and burned stones that were once their beloved city would have been heartbreaking. The spiritual condition was just as depressing. Isaiah described this as a thick darkness coving the earth (Isa. 60:2). Yet, just as the sun rises over the rubble of the formerly magnificent urban skyline and the early morning light is replaced by the full brightness of the sun, God's glory shines on the city.

Isaiah's vision of the restored Jerusalem is both now and not yet. There were aspects that would be fulfilled in the actual rebuilding of Jerusalem. At the same time a hint of the ultimate transformation in the New Jerusalem is also seen. God's glory will one day replace the sun and moon as sources of light.

Shortly after a fire destroyed a large section of my community, a local graffiti artist painted a mural with the words "Rise up Botocan." The mural was so appreciated that the local government sponsored a contest for graffiti artists to paint murals throughout the community. The beautifully painted walls provided a glimmer of beauty as we struggled through a season of piles of burned debris and several months without electricity.

God has acted to transform the city. Linthicum writes, "God has created, loved, preserved, and redeemed the city so that it can be transformed into the city God intends it to be."[53] Isaiah described how the rebuilding would impact daily life. The city will be made beautiful, become a destination for migration, grow economically, experience peace, and inspire hope for future improvements.

Isaiah 60 is a vision of the overall transformation of Jerusalem with a special focus on beauty. The passage begins with light, which is needed to see beauty. There is a call to "Lift up your eyes all around, and see" (Isa. 60:4). The beauty was already there. What they needed was the ability to see the beauty around them.

Isaiah emphasized the city being made beautiful (Isa. 60:7, 9, 13). God started the process of beautifying his house. The beauty of the temple was one way to point worshipers to the glory of God. Beauty has value in and of itself. A city that is transforming is also becoming physically attractive. A city can be made beautiful through its buildings, streets, parks, plazas, and the overall layout of the area.

Beauty is in nature as created by God and also in the creation of people through artistic expressions. Injustice and oppression are distortions of the creative ability of people and therefore result in ugliness. The pains of poverty are ugly. Malnourished children are not pleasant to look at. It is only after they have been cared for and restored to health that their beauty is fully exposed. Communities that have been ravaged by war, poverty, or neglect are not as beautiful as they should be. Transformation restores their beauty to make it easier to see and appreciate.

Beautification must include both aesthetic improvements and the ability to see the beauty that already exists within a community. Beautifying a community can result in much more than surface level changes. It is true that painting a rotten wall will not prevent it from falling down.

Beautification must go hand in hand with other approaches of engagement. And yet, it cannot be ignored.

Beauty is often omitted from the designs of low-income communities. Communities that are block after block of the same bland housing design can feel depressing and expose one of the many flaws of failed attempts at providing affordable housing for the poor. Dullness is ugliness. Jane Jacobs describes this neighborhood design as monotonous. She writes:

> In places stamped with the monotony and repetition of sameness you move, but in moving you seem to have got nowhere. North is the same as south, or east as west. Sometimes north, south, east, and west are all alike, as they are when you stand within the grounds of a large project . . . Monotony of this sort is generally considered too oppressive to be pursued as an ideal by everybody but some project planners or the most routine-minded real-estate developers.[54]

Renowned author Leo Tolstoy reflects on the social importance of art. He writes art "is a means of union among men, joining them together in the same feelings, and indispensable for the life and progress toward well-being of individuals and of humanity."[55] Beauty is not a sideline component of community life. According to Tolstoy it is indispensable for transforming communities.

My mission organization, Servant Partners, recognizes the role of beauty in community transformation by having beauty and creativity as one of its nine signs of transformation. "In a transforming community beauty, creativity, and artistic expression flourish on an individual and communal level in a way that serves individuals and the community as a whole."[56] Beauty is seen in transforming people and neighborhoods.

Conversely, the beautification of a city has been used as an excuse to oppress the poor. Slums are considered eyesores and demolished for the simple reason that people of wealth and power do not like the way they look. Oppressive building codes add extra hardship on the poor, so the upper classes do not have to see poverty. I have seen informal settlements along roads that were required to paint their outer wall the same color to hide their poverty from wealthy motorists.

Beauty and transformation must cater to the marginalized. A beautiful city is one that does not hide poverty. Nor does it marginalize the poor by only beautifying the districts of the elite. Places of beauty in the city need to be free and accessible to all of the city's residents so that the beauty of a city is not limited to a luxury of the rich.

The beautification of a city is a manifestation of transformation. The opposite is already established. The connection between litter, graffiti, and general urban decay are clear. People care less about their surroundings when they think that other people don't care either. A neighborhood deprived of beauty undercuts the motivation to work for improvements. Perkins writes, "Living in an ugly environment is depressing and makes us less likely to care about that environment. Some urban children are growing up without an appreciation for beauty because they see so few examples of it."[57] The beautification of a community can function as a catalyst for other changes.

Beautification can help local residents to have a better quality of life. Montgomery writes, "The frequent sight of garbage, graffiti, and disrepair produces alienation and depression, especially among seniors. We know from research on biophilia that infusions of nature don't merely calm the mind, they alter our attitudes, making us more trusting and generous toward other people."[58] Beautification is an important aspect of transformation that goes well beyond aesthetics.

While picking up trash and removing graffiti is a start, the mere absence of ugliness is not a substitute for beautification. Beautification can include a wide range of expressions. Art can be used in transformation in a variety of ways. Art for empowerment is through learning artistic skills. My wife has taught nail art, fondant cakes, and calligraphy to some of the women in our community. A few of them have used their skills as a way to earn extra money. Most have added beauty to their lives as they honed their skills.

Art is an effective tool for advocacy and public awareness. It helps with reflection and critical thinking and has the power to express without limits. I have used art to reflect on social issues. The simple exercise of drawing your community as you see it can bring out insights and biases regarding how you view your neighborhood. A great comparative exercise is to draw your community, as you believe God wants it to be based on one of the prophetic visions of transformation. This reveals your desires for how you want to see your community transformed.

Beauty can be found in all forms of artistic expression from traditional art to drama, dance, music, writing, and many other forms. Involvement in the arts can help restore people's dignity as they exercise their creative imagination. A community that is transforming will become more beautiful as people find their voice through creative expression.

Reflection and Action

1. What can you do to work for the beautification of your community?
2. How is God glorified through expressions of beauty in your city?
3. Take five photos of things that are beautiful in your community.

Chapter 36

Urban Transformation and Missions: Reflections on Amos 9:11-15

"In that day I will raise up the booth of David that is fallen and repair its breaches, and raise up its ruins and rebuild it as in the days of old, that they may possess the remnant of Edom and all the nations who are called by my name," declares the LORD who does this. "Behold, the days are coming," declares the LORD, "when the plowman shall overtake the reaper and the treader of grapes him who sows the seed; the mountains shall drip sweet wine, and all the hills shall flow with it. I will restore the fortunes of my people Israel, and they shall rebuild the ruined cities and inhabit them; they shall plant vineyards and drink their wine, and they shall make gardens and eat their fruit. I will plant them on their land, and they shall never again be uprooted out of the land that I have given them," says the LORD your God (Amos 9:11-15).

Historical Background

Amos prophesied during the reigns of Uzziah, king of Judah (783-742 BC), and Jeroboam II, king of Israel (786-746 BC) (Amos 1:1, see also 2 Kings 14:23-15:7 and 2 Chron. 26). This was during the pre-exilic period when Assyria began expanding its empire. At first, Israel was able to enlarge her borders because Assyria weakened her northern neighbors but had not yet become a threat to Israel or Judah. The economic growth was concentrated on the top as the elites of Israel became wealthy at the expense of the poor.

Israel's oppression of the poor went hand in hand with its spiritual decay. Biblical scholars Billy Smith and Frank Page write:

> The period was characterized by moral and spiritual decline and by social upheaval. Israel's frequent attendance at the shrines to make sacrifices did not result in moral, spiritual, and social uprightness. The rich oppressed the poor, indulged in extravagant lifestyles, denied justice to the oppressed, and engaged in immoral sexual activities (2:6-8; 4:1; 5:11-13).[59]

God's law spoke against such injustices. False gods who approved of oppressing the poor replaced the worship of the true God. Idolatry and oppression of the poor reached epidemic proportions during the time of Amos.

Urban Transformation and Missions

Many of the members of Balic-Balic Christian Church became passionate about starting outreach Bible studies in other communities. Their church was planted years before when missionaries moved into their community and taught about Jesus. After those original members matured in their faith, they became the ones to go and teach others about Jesus. Through their efforts a house church and several home Bible studies were started where people were coming to faith and being discipled. Even after Balic-Balic Christian Church was destroyed in a government-sponsored demolition, the house church and outreach Bible studies continued.

After nine chapters of warnings of upcoming judgment because of idolatry and oppression of the poor, Amos closes with a message of hope. This hope is not simply the rebuilding of one city, but the whole nation. It is a vision of nation-building with an emphasis on rebuilding cities.

The political system will be restored with David's dynasty being raised up. This would ensure justice in the land. Oppression and idolatry will cease under the reign of a just and righteous king.

The religious system of true worship of Yahweh will be restored. The nations who are called by the name of Yahweh will be under his reign. The people of God will walk in obedience.

The economic system of abundance and a just distribution will be restored. "'Behold, the days are coming,' declares the LORD, 'when the plowman shall overtake the reaper and the treader of grapes him who sows the seed; the mountains shall drip sweet wine, and all the hills shall flow with it'" (Amos 9:13). The image Amos presents is one of great abundance. Crops are growing and producing fruit as fast as they are planted. The workers are barely able to keep up. This abundant produce does not simply enrich the elite while the rest of the nation remains in poverty. The workers will receive just compensation for their labor. The cities they rebuild will be the same cities they live in. The vineyards they plant and harvest will produce the same wine they drink. The gardens they plant and tend will be the same gardens they eat from.

Amos' vision of urban transformation was also one of missions. Amos looks to a time when the people of God are not limited to the nation of Israel (Amos 9:11-12). All the nations will one day worship God.

The church in Antioch was the fulfillment of Amos' vision, with the shift from a *come and see* to a *go and tell* approach to missions. Antioch was a multiethnic church that had a vision to send workers to tell the nations about Christ (Acts 13:1-3). Bakke writes, the "Antioch Church invented foreign mission—*but not when they sent two of their pastors away*. They invented it when they were reconciling the diversity of the city into a common fellowship in Jesus Christ and when they were reaching out to the needy with hunger offerings before they went out with gospel offerings."[60] The transformation that brought different ethnic groups to worship resulted in sending out their best.

James refers to Amos 9:11-12 during the Jerusalem Council when he states that the prophets agree with Gentiles coming to faith (Acts 15:15-17). James does not limit his meaning to Amos. He uses the plural of prophets, meaning multiple prophets. The prophets as a whole agree that the nations will one day worship God.

Paul and the early church experienced the nations coming to faith in their mission strategy of focusing on cities. The urban centers came to faith in Jesus and they turned their world upside down (Acts 17:6). Ministry in today's cities has the potential to see the nations come to faith. Bakke emphasizes the importance of cities in modern missions.

> Mission is no longer about crossing the oceans, jungles and deserts, but about crossing the streets of the world's cities. From now on, nearly all ministry will be crosscultural amid the urban pluralism caused by the greatest migration in human history from Southern hemispheres to the North, from East to West and, above all, from rural to urban.[61]

Churches can never be purely internally focused. There is always the component of looking outward. Churches need to have the mindset of missions. They need to continually pray and work to see those around them come to faith in Jesus and grow in Christ. They also need to have a continual focus on sending their members to do long-term ministry.

Urban transformation and missions both complement each other. Metro-Manila is in the transformation process and has made great strides in many areas. The air quality of the city has noticeably improved over the years. Health care is available and relatively affordable even for the poor. Well-paying jobs are available for skilled professionals and the uneducated at least have some employment options. The church is strong and growing. People are coming to faith in Jesus and are passionate about loving God with their whole hearts and their neighbors as themselves.

High-quality Bible schools and seminaries are training church leaders with an emphasis on missions and transformation. Churches throughout the city are mission-minded and have commissioned some of their members for cross-cultural ministry. There is a growing passion to see the name of Jesus proclaimed to the nations.

Reflection and Action

1. Describe your church's work of evangelism and discipleship in your community.
2. What can you do to mobilize your church for cross-cultural ministry?

Section V

Hope

Chapter 37

Dreaming of a Better Future: Reflections on Jeremiah 31:23-26

> Thus says the LORD of hosts, the God of Israel: "Once more they shall use these words in the land of Judah and in its cities, when I restore their fortunes: 'The LORD bless you, O habitation of righteousness, O holy hill!' And Judah and all its cities shall dwell there together, and the farmers and those who wander with their flocks. For I will satisfy the weary soul, and every languishing soul I will replenish." At this I awoke and looked, and my sleep was pleasant to me (Jeremiah 31:23-26).

The Word of the Lord came to Jeremiah in a series of five messages while he was sleeping. Jeremiah received God's promise of holistic transformation (Jer. 30:1). The fortunes of the nation will be restored (Jer. 30:3). God will heal their wounds (Jer. 30:17). Jerusalem will be rebuilt (Jer. 30:18). The people will return to their homeland (Jer. 31:17). After Jeremiah received God's word he awoke from a pleasant sleep.

Jeremiah dreamed that God would restore the fortunes of Judah and its cities. This brought back to use an old proverb of Jerusalem. "The LORD bless you, O habitation of righteousness, O holy hill!" (Jer. 31:23). The proverb describes the city as a home of righteousness and a holy hill. It is where the people know God and have been forgiven (Jer. 31:34).

Jeremiah began his message to the people in response to his dream by stressing the sovereign control of God. God destroys but he also rebuilds and plants. He will free his people from their current exile and allow them to return to their beloved homeland.

God will watch over them as they build and plant. The rebuilding is according to his desire. It is within his will. God assures his blessings on the work of their hand by watching over the rebuilding of cities and the planting of crops.

Satisfied in God So We Can Dream of a Better Future

Jeremiah wrote the word of the Lord, "For I will satisfy the weary soul, and every languishing soul I will replenish" (Jer. 31:25). Within the context of Jeremiah's message of restoration, he wrote of God, "I will feast the soul of the priests with abundance, and my people shall be satisfied with my goodness, declares the LORD" (Jer. 31:14). In God is true satisfaction. Being satisfied in God allows us to take our focus off of our problems and look to the greatness of God. Dreaming of better cities starts with seeing God and not simply the problems of our communities.

Years ago, I learned what it is to be truly satisfied in God. I took a wealthy student to visit the railroad community of Balic-Balic, Manila. Walking along railroad tracks we passed hundreds of people as they went about their daily routine. We stopped at the home of Emma and her family. Their small 200 square feet home housed five people. It had no running water and leaked in multiple places. The rats scampered across the rafters as we talked.

We sat and listened to Emma share about her life growing up in an informal settlement. She showed us the plastic stapled to the ceiling to catch the drips when it rains. We heard stories about Emma having to eat rice with salt, oil, or ketchup when there was no other food available. She shared her struggles to get through classes without eating and not knowing how she would pay for school supplies. We also heard how God had transformed her life as a young girl when she accepted Jesus. Her life before Jesus is described as hopeless, while life with Jesus is hopeful.

While listening to her casually talk about her life, I noticed the wealthy student's eyes turning red and beginning to water. We ended our visit and I escorted our visitor out of the community. Hearing the stories of the hardships and struggles of life in poverty brought tears to this student's eyes.

A few days later, I spoke to Emma about the experience. I commented that the student was tearing up. Emma also noticed it and replied, "She doesn't need to cry for me because I know Jesus. She should cry for those who don't know Jesus." This is coming from someone who is in destitute poverty and lacks even the basic necessities of having enough food for the day. Yet, she is fully satisfied in God. Jesus is her hope, not food or any other need. Instead of self-pity she is joyful about life because of her relationship with Jesus.

Emma's satisfaction in Jesus allowed her to dream of a better community. She rejected the temptation of wealth and chose not to move permanently to the United States even though she had the opportunity to do so. After living in the United States for almost two years, Emma moved back into the same informal settlement she grew up in. She dreamed of sharing the hope she has in Jesus with her neighbors who live in hopelessness.[62]

Dreaming of Better Cities

One of the devastating effects of poverty is hopelessness. When someone believes that their poverty is inevitable or even deserved it undercuts any effort to improve a community. Dreaming of a better future includes being able to see that God can transform communities regardless of their current condition. For communities to improve, it takes someone who dreams of transformation.

The more a neighborhood spirals downward in decay, the harder it is to have hope for the future. During a difficult season, my community faced one hardship after another. A fire destroyed fifteen homes and damaged many others. Stricter laws regarding drugs meant a significant increase in police raids in the community. Police brutality became commonplace to the point where they were feared and considered the enemies of the neighborhood. Violence was becoming increasingly common. There were several murders including a hired assassin killing a police informant. On top of all this, the government began to threaten to raze the community and relocate the residents outside the city.

Living in the midst of those hardships meant that every ounce of emotional energy was going into making it through another day. At the end of the day I had nothing left to imagine the community improving. The problems had become so immense that hopelessness crept in. Dreaming of a better future was almost impossible.

In contrast, when my family moved to a different neighborhood, we entered a community that was full of hope. I soon realized that most people liked where they lived. It was not a place that people dreamed of moving from. It was where they were achieving their dreams of building a better future for themselves and their families.

Dreaming of a better community is one of the gifts of the youth in my neighborhood. The parents and grandparents who migrated to the city tend to have an idealistic view of the countryside and a negative view of their current neighborhood. The younger generation has a positive view of their community. It is not a place they want to leave even if they can afford to move out. There is hope that the future will get better.

Transformation starts with a dream that by faith change is possible. When we relocated to an informal settlement we did not know what was going to happen. We had a dream to plant a church that would love God and engage the community for transformation. God blessed that dream and we have had the joy of seeing the fruit of a church whose members love God and love their neighbors.

Reflection and Action

1. Ask God what he wants for your community.

2. Draw a "dream map" of your community showing it as you dream it might one day become.

Chapter 38

Finding Hope in an Urban Wasteland

Reflections on Zechariah 1:14-17

So the angel who talked with me said to me, 'Cry out, Thus says the LORD of hosts: I am exceedingly jealous for Jerusalem and for Zion. And I am exceedingly angry with the nations that are at ease; for while I was angry but a little, they furthered the disaster. Therefore, thus says the LORD, I have returned to Jerusalem with mercy; my house shall be built in it, declares the LORD of hosts, and the measuring line shall be stretched out over Jerusalem. Cry out again, Thus says the LORD of hosts: My cities shall again overflow with prosperity, and the LORD will again comfort Zion and again choose Jerusalem' (Zechariah 1:14-17).

Zechariah was a post-exilic prophet writing during the time when the exiles had returned from Babylon. Zechariah had eight visions in the night, the first of which were horsemen who went throughout the earth (Zech. 1:7-17).

The people of Jerusalem during the time of Zechariah were in a place of pain. They were living in an urban wasteland. The city's walls were destroyed, and the temple was in ruins. The only nice buildings were the mansions of the elite. Everyone else essentially lived in skid row.

Today's cities can also be places of pain. "Dominique! Dominque! Don't fall asleep!" These were the shouts outside my window at one in the morning. There are sometimes shouts outside my window at all hours of the night, so I soon fell back to sleep. The next morning, I learned the shouts were from Dominique's wife who was helping him get to a hospital. A neighbor was offended by one of Dominique's comments, so he stabbed him. Dominique died before reaching the hospital. In an instant his young wife became a widow and his two small children were fatherless.

Dominique's murder happened in the same community where we have seen God work so many times, and experienced so much fruit. The killing is a painful reminder of how much work still needs to be done to see my beloved community transformed.

After seeing a vision of horsemen sent to patrol the earth, Zechariah encountered an angel. The angel gave Zechariah a message of hope for him to proclaim in a place of pain. God announced his jealousy for Jerusalem (Zech. 1:14). God was jealous because the people had broken their covenant with him. God promised to return to Jerusalem with mercy, and that his house would be rebuilt. The cities of Judah would once again be prosperous, and Jerusalem will be God's city.

The temple was not the only building to be rebuilt, since a measuring line would be stretched over the entire city. The measuring line symbolically represented the start of the rebuilding process. The measuring line was used to mark the boundaries of the new wall. The rebuilding had begun with God before the construction workers actually begin. The rebuilding was itself a message of hope since it signified the return of God's favor and the restoration of the economy.

Hope and Transformation

Rebuilt cities, renewed cities, and restored cities all speak of hope. Their hope was in a great and glorious God who makes all things new. Hope recognizes that the future will be better than the current situation of despair. There is hope that our broken and decayed cities will be transformed. There is hope for the homeless living on the streets. Hope for the small business owner trying to stay afloat. Hope for parents raising children in the midst of many challenges. Hope for those who are stuck in traffic and late for work. There is hope that change is possible.

Hope is powerful. Paul wrote to the Corinthians, "Does he not certainly speak for our sake? It was written for our sake, because the plowman should plow in hope and the thresher thresh in hope of sharing in the crop" (1 Cor. 9:10). Within the context of his rights as an apostle, Paul looked at the example of farmers hopeful for a productive crop at harvest time as the motivation for plowing and threshing. Hope can mean the difference between wallowing in self-pity or passionately loving God with our whole being and loving our neighbor as ourselves.

Jerusalem was still an urban wasteland but God "will again comfort Zion" (Zech. 1:17). God has redeemed them. There is hope in the rubble and ash of the destroyed city because there is hope in God. Zechariah sought to help the returned exiles break out of their fatalistic depression by giving them hope for their city.

Hope is a glorious gift from God. With hope, the current situation can be viewed as temporary. Regardless of how bad the situation is hope sees change as possible. Nightmare political leaders will not permanently oppress the people. Drug dealers and gang activity are not permanent. The most bombed out shell of a city can be rebuilt to become a place of peace.

Hope in the power of God to transform their community led the residents of an informal settlement to not give up even after their community was reduced to ash. A fire had broken out in the evening and destroyed a large section of their community. The residents immediately began rebuilding. Most families built with cement instead of wood so that a future fire would not spread. A working fire protection system was also put in place. The post-fire neighborhood was not only rebuilt, it is now safer from the risk of fire than it previously had been. The residents have hope and they rebuilt a better community.

Hope encourages the poor to put effort into improving their lives and communities. Over many years my community has slowly improved. The area was once a vacant lot overgrown with weeds when the first residents began to move in. At that time there were no government services and the residents were ever cautious of being evicted and their possessions confiscated. They lived in makeshift tents constructed of scrap wood and rice sacks. Over time their confidence grew because no one bothered them for living there. Family members from the countryside were invited to move in and the population grew. Homes were constructed of more permanent materials and services such as water, electricity, and garbage collection were brought to the community. Dirt walkways were paved so the residents no longer have to walk in mud when it rains. The neighborhood has been on the road of transformation for many years but there is still much work to be done.

Even in the face of insurmountable odds the residents have persevered. Fire is only one of many obstacles faced by the residents. At one time, the local government had demolished a small portion of the community. A large wall was built creating a boundary between the poor and an upper class subdivision. In the midst of all of the setbacks the community has not lost hope. Many of the residents are proud of their community and remain hopeful that their lives will continue to improve.

There is a sense of hopefulness in the community. This hope can be seen in the lives of students who attend classes even when they have to go the whole day without eating. Hope is in the seemingly endless construction projects as residents continually upgrade their homes and businesses. Hope is in the laughter of children playing simple tag games with friends. Hope is in the opening of businesses as families take concrete steps to improve their lives. Hope is seen in the residents' desire to see their community transformed as opposed to simply dreaming of moving out.

Reflection and Action

1. What are the signs of hope in your community?
2. What can you do to be hopeful even if your circumstances seem grim?

Chapter 39

Community Celebration: Reflections on Zechariah 2:1-13

> Sing and rejoice, O daughter of Zion, for behold, I come and I will dwell in your midst, declares the LORD (Zechariah 2:10).

Zechariah's third vision was a man with a measuring line examining the size of Jerusalem (Zech. 2:1-2). An angel explained that the city's population would outgrow the walls. The economy of the city would be so strong that the multitude of cattle would also be too large to fit inside the old city. The defensive wall around the city would become obsolete because the city will outgrow its original size. Yet, they will still be protected since God himself would be the city's wall (Zech. 2:3-5).

The vision of the restoration of Jerusalem signified the end of the exile. The nations would no longer be God's instrument of judgment. Instead they will join themselves to the Lord and become his people (Zech. 2:11). Jerusalem was to become a multiethnic community.

The population growth, economic recovery, and God claiming the city as his home contributed to the transformation of the city. The physical rebuilding by the man with the measuring line was just one part of the larger restoration of the city.

Celebrating Urban Transformation

A group of pastors and church workers studying Transformational Urban Leadership in a master's program at Asian Theological Seminary gathered at an eco-farm for a time of rest and celebration. We reflected on the Israelites' journey from slavery to liberation and related Scripture to God's work in our different ministries. We ended the gathering with a time of worship and celebration. We were celebrating life and the transformation happening in each of our ministries.

Community wide celebration of the work of God in rebuilding ruined cities is a theme throughout the prophets. Zechariah called the city's residents to sing for joy and be glad (Zech. 2:10). The reason for the celebration was the coming of God to dwell in their midst. The rebuilding of the city, the population growth, and the improved economy were all good things, but it was God's presence behind the more visible forms of transformation that was the real reason to celebrate.

Isaiah spoke of the residents of Jerusalem rejoicing in the restoration of their city (Isa. 66:10-11). After experiencing God's work of transformation, the people of Jerusalem were to rejoice with the renewed city. They were to be glad for her. There was to be genuine joy for the work of God in the city. Isaiah also wrote, "And the ransomed of the LORD shall return and come to Zion with singing; everlasting joy shall be upon their heads; they shall obtain gladness and joy, and sorrow and sighing shall flee away" (Isa. 51:11). The return from exile and the rebuilding of Jerusalem would be a joyful time.

Jeremiah, the weeping prophet, speaks of the voice of gladness over God's transformational work (Jer. 33:11). Jeremiah wrote that from the rebuilt city "shall come songs of thanksgiving, and the voices of those who celebrate" (Jer. 30:19). The improvement of a community brings about joy and a reason to celebrate.

Singing of God's Transforming Work

I am always encouraged by the informal jam sessions in our church. I can hear the spontaneous worship from my house, which is on the second floor of the same building. Those that can play instruments use whatever is available while the rest sing. They are excited about life and express their joy through songs. The impromptu worship times are rooted in faith and struggle as the youth turn to God in praise.

Singing of God's transformative work is found in the rich history of the people of God. After David built his palace in Jerusalem, he had the ark brought to the city (1 Chron. 15-16). The ark had been the symbol of God's presence and was now being placed once again in God's chosen city. The people had hope that God was in their midst. This was a cause for celebration. "So all Israel brought up the ark of the covenant of the LORD with shouting, to the sound of the horn, trumpets, and cymbals, and made loud music on harps and lyres" (1 Chron. 15:28).

David celebrated but not as dignified royalty. David leaped for joy and sponsored a massive feast giving food to everyone in Israel (1 Chron. 16:3). Finally, David gives thanks to God in song (1 Chron. 16:8-36). David expressed thankfulness to God for protecting the nation from oppressors. He also calls the earth to sing praises to God for he is to be worshiped as the God who reigns.

The Psalmist continued the theme of singing praises to God for his work of rebuilding cities. "Let heaven and earth praise him, the seas and everything that moves in them. For God will save Zion and build up the cities of Judah, and people shall dwell there and possess it; the offspring of his servants shall inherit it, and those who love his name shall dwell in it" (Ps. 69:34-36).

In a Psalm of Ascent, the pilgrims traveling to Jerusalem to worship God sang, "Unless the LORD builds the house, those who build it labor in vain. Unless the LORD watches over the city, the watchman stays awake in vain" (Ps. 127:1). God is credited as the one who both builds houses and watches over the city. The whole process of transformation is the work of God.

Psalms 113-118 were sung during the celebration of Passover. These songs centered on celebrating God's work of liberating oppressed slaves from a powerful empire. This community celebration of remembering God's work in the past was a source of praise and joy.

After the wall was completed and the city was repopulated, Nehemiah dedicated the wall of Jerusalem. The dedication was celebrated with gladness and songs (Neh. 12:27). They formed two choirs that marched in different locations around the city and met at the temple. The whole city had a parade and street festival to thank God for the successful completion of the city's wall.

The return of God's favor upon the city was the reason for the community to celebrate. "Sing and rejoice, O daughter of Zion, for behold, I come and I will dwell in your midst, declares the LORD" (Zech. 2:10). They were to sing and rejoice; both of which are actions of celebration. The command captures the excitement felt when experiencing the presence of God.

Transforming communities is the work of God. While there is a limit to human action, God's power is limitless. The fruit of all effort to improve our neighborhoods is the work of God. God's transformational work should be celebrated with singing and rejoicing. "Sing aloud, O daughter of Zion; shout, O Israel! Rejoice and exult with all your heart, O daughter of Jerusalem!" (Zep. 3:14).

Reflection and Action

1. What are the reasons to celebrate in your community?
2. What songs express joy in the work of God in your community?
3. Sing praises to God for his work in your community.

Chapter 40

Encouragement for Rebuilders of Ruined Cities: Reflections on 1 and 2 Chronicles

> And David lived in the stronghold; therefore it was called the city of David. And he built the city all around from the Millo in complete circuit, and Joab repaired the rest of the city (1 Chronicles 11:7-8).

First and Second Chronicles were written to provide hope and encouragement for the returned exiles as they struggled to restore their nation and rebuild their capital city. Bakke writes, "The books called Chronicles emerged from documents compiled by folks combing through the ruins of destroyed cities after the captivity and exile in Babylon."[63] First and Second Chronicles can be dated around the time of Ezra and Nehemiah in the midst of the rebuilding effort.

Emphasis on the Positive

History can be studied from the perspective of what was great about a people's past, or how horrible they were. The need to rebuild ruined cities shaped the view of history presented in Chronicles. The leaders are portrayed in a more positive light than in Kings. The exiles did not need to focus on the war between Saul and David, or David's sin with Bathsheba. They did not need to be reminded of Solomon's oppressive policies or his foreign wives.

The people already knew that their ancestors had turned from God in sin. This point was driven home to them every day of their lives as they struggled to rebuild. The last thing they needed was more details of the sins of their forefathers. What they needed to realize was that their ancestors were not pure evil. Even the most sinful among them, such as King Manasseh, had times in their lives when they turned toward God. Instead of focusing on shortcomings, Chronicles reminds them that they were the descendants of many great people who worshiped an even greater God.

In order to be able to see the potential around them, the returned exiles needed a sense of belonging. While biblical genealogies tend to be boring for modern readers, the genealogies painstakingly recorded in Chronicles encouraged the exiles to rebuild by showing the rich heritage of the people. They were not a random group of people. They were the descendants of David and his mighty men. They were a respected people with much to be proud of.

The exiles were not merely a group of conquered peoples sent back to an urban wasteland to suffer worse than they did in Babylon. Their present condition of destruction and defeat was not who they were as a people. They were the people of God with a history and heroes. They belonged in Jerusalem, but not the destroyed burned down Jerusalem. They belonged in the city of God that would be rebuilt beyond its historical greatness.

Chronicles also focuses on the positive by showing that the nation had a long history of building cities. It is in their blood. The great leaders David and Joab were credited with rebuilding Jerusalem after they captured the city (1 Chron. 10:7-8). Solomon and Rehoboam had extensive city-building projects (2 Chron. 8:1-6, 11:5-12). They built whole new cities and fortified existing ones. Jotham's kingship is recognized for his work on the temple and building cities (2 Chron. 27:1-4).

There is a close connection between religious reforms and building cities. King Asa built cities in conjunction with removing the places associated with the worship of false gods (2 Chron. 14:5-7). King Jehoshaphat removed the places of false worship and had Levites teach the Law of the Lord throughout all the cities in Judah. He also built fortress and store cities in Judah (2 Chron. 17:1-19). Manasseh, who is better known for his sins than his reforms, did have a period of reforms that was also connected to city-building (2 Chron. 33:12-15).

God blessed their ancestors with the creativity, resources, and ability to expand and build cities. Now the returned exiles were in the position to act as urban rebuilders.

Eyes to See What Works in our Communities

Seeing the potential of a rundown neighborhood is not always easy. Nathanael's question, "Can anything good come out of Nazareth?" (John 1:46) can be asked about a lot of places. The natural way to view a community is to look for its problems. This is especially true of low-income neighborhoods because we are socially conditioned to see them as problem-infested slums. The word slum itself tends to bring up images of squalor, crime, and violence.

Eyes to see what works in our communities takes a paradigm shift in the way we approach our communities. We must intentionally look for positive aspects in our communities. When we put effort into looking for what's good, all of a sudden we begin to see our neighborhoods in a new light. We begin to realize that there are aspects of our communities that actually function well.

When I first moved into Botocan, I spent months walking around asking residents what they wanted to improve about their community. Instead of talking about what they wanted to change, everyone seemed to share what they liked about it. I heard comments such as, "We're informal settlers, but we're different. We're orderly and good." It took a while, but I finally realized that I was the one with the problem. I had been conditioned to assume that because the community was an informal settlement it would be full of problems. At that time, I had no concept of concentrating on what worked. I came to the realization that I needed to change my approach. Instead of looking for problems I began looking for what was good about my community.

I started by looking at what other churches and ministries were doing in my community. I learned that the other church in Botocan was in a period of growth. They had seen many people come to faith and were growing in their walk with Jesus. I began to see how the Holy Spirit was at work in my community.

The more I looked, the more I began to discover other assets. The residents themselves built this community, so it was built based on their needs. I began to realize that the community design itself helps the poor improve their lives.

I spent a day counting all of the different businesses in my community. The amount of business activity is staggering. There are about 1,300 buildings and over 300 businesses in my community. It is not only the number of business establishments, but also the variety that helps my community to function well. Basic goods and services can be found within my community. There is no need to spend time and money commuting to commercial establishments in other parts of the city. I can buy most things I need within a short walk from my home such as groceries, freshly made bread, school supplies for my children, and even passport photos.

There are so many assets in my community; it is worth mentioning that I live in an informal settlement in a developing world megacity. Of course, there are plenty of problems. They are still there, but by looking at what works we are able to develop a balanced perspective of our neighborhoods.

A great way to see what works in our communities is by creating an asset map. Asset maps can focus on all of the assets to give a big picture view of what's working in a community. They can also be specific to one asset, such as mapping all of the businesses, neighborhood associations, or churches in a community. An asset map can focus on the infrastructure of a community or even the physical environment such as parks, land for community gardens, and the location of the community. The skills, talents, and education levels of the residents themselves can also be mapped as an asset.

Asset maps can focus on a variety of areas to help us see what works in our communities.

I often have short-term teams that stay in my community spend a morning walking around a small section of the neighborhood and drawing an asset map based on their observations. They are always surprised at how many good things they end up seeing. The simple exercise of walking through a community in order to intentionally look for things that work is a powerful tool for changing how we see our communities.

Reflection and Action

1. What stories from your city's history can provide encouragement for future transformation?
2. Draw an asset map of your community.

Chapter 41

What Shall We Do?

The prophetic visions of rebuilding ruined cities provide us with a variety of signs of urban transformation. These signs are not intended to be all-inclusive, but they can provide lights along the path helping us to know where we are going.

Working for Holistic Transformation

Lasting improvement in the lives of a city's residents, particularly the most vulnerable in society, does not usually happen by addressing single issues. The issues of the city are so extensive they must be addressed holistically. Transformation by its very definition is holistic. The prophets gave the broken people of God words of hope that included the comprehensive restoration of their beloved city.

Holistic transformation is working for the overall improvement of a community. At the same time, it is also not trying do everything. It recognizes that what you are doing is not the whole picture, and therefore, the work of others is important. When I was looking for a community to move into in order to plant a church, one of the reasons we chose Botocan was that the only church in the community at that time was very excited about the idea of planting another church. Before we started a new church we emphasized that we would be located in a different section of the community and have a different ministry focus. Other ministries, NGOs, and the local government are also involved in different areas that when combined, show a picture of working towards holistic transformation.

A Passion for the Word of God

Central to the prophetic visions of urban transformation is the glory of God. Everything we do should be about God and for his glory. Praising God for his work in our communities comes from knowing him through the study of Scripture. As we saw from the prophetic passages studied in this book, the Bible addresses the complex issues of today's urban context.

The Bible can give us hope that God cares about our broken cities and hears our prayers for our neighborhoods. We need to develop a passion for the Word of God. We need to study the Word, know the Word, and live the Word. We must become so saturated in Scripture that it shapes our thinking and worldview. It is then that we can love God with our whole being and love our neighbors as ourselves. The Bible gives us the strength and courage to work to make our communities better places to live.

Holistic Discipleship

An individualistic faith that only focuses on personal morality was not how Jesus taught his followers to live. Our discipleship today must emphasize loving God with our whole being and loving our neighbors as ourselves. A key aspect of loving our neighbors includes addressing the issues of injustice and oppression.

The devastating effect of discipleship that omits the deeper issues of justice and mercy came to full horrifying light in the Rwandan genocide. Before the tragic events of 1994, Rwanda experienced wave after wave of revivals that saw church growth explode by the hundreds of thousands. For all practical purposes Rwanda had been reached and was considered a "Christian" nation.

Externally everything looked good, but the bonds of ethnic barriers were never addressed in discipleship. Christians brutally butchered fellow Christians of a different ethnicity. Activist Craig Greenfield writes, "In a Christianized nation, Christians killed Christians. In a country where only a tiny minority did not identify themselves as Christian, injustice and chaos reigned because ethnic designations—Hutu or Tutsi—were considered more important than a shared Christian identity."[64] Shallow evangelism that only cares about filling churches is not obedience to the command of the Great Commission to make disciples.

This tragic event should never be repeated. We need a holistic discipleship that will break all human barriers and love neighbors regardless of race, ethnicity, nationality, religion, political alignment, social class, or any other area that makes someone different.

The prophetic visions of urban transformation reflected upon in this book are about loving God and loving others through engaging our world by working for justice. Pop-Christianity that allows someone to become a Christian without any significant lifestyle change must be rejected. Christ must become King in our lives. He must reign over our employment, where we live, how we use money, and how we spend our free time. Confronting oppression and injustice and seeking to glorify God through loving others, particularly the poor, are important aspects of faith in Jesus.

Start Where You Are

A journey of 1,000 miles starts with the first step. Rebuilding ruined cities begins where you are. It does not have to be large or great. When thousands of small acts of love are combined, a movement begins that has the power to transform society.

Starting where you are can be as simple as a meal. I will close with the reflection of my friend Ina who shared her experience of eating a meal with a homeless family.

> Yesterday afternoon a friend and I met Rita while we were walking. We had a packed lunch and were looking for a place to sit down to eat when we noticed a homeless woman and her children separating trash on the side of the road. Awkwardly, we approached the homeless family and asked if we could eat lunch with them. They were overjoyed by the offer and ate immediately.
>
> From our conversation we learned that Rita is a 41 year-old single mom with three children. She has been homeless for more than 10 years. Her ex-husband lost his job as a construction worker and started to physically

abuse Rita and the children. Eventually she left him and moved to the city with their children.

As we talked, I looked into her eyes and thin body. I believe she does not have enough food to eat. Rita's eyes watered when she talked. "Most of the people from my hometown came to the city with a dream of a better life, but unfortunately this city is not fulfilling our dreams. And yet, for me and my children, this kind of life is enough, at least our life is happy."

Rita continued her story, "To be honest, I do not like this homeless type of living, it's shameful. I want a house and a better life, but what kind of life is there if the government does not provide jobs. I do not believe the government anymore, they just please the rich and kill the poor."

I noticed her children were working to separate the garbage. Rita and her children are very creative and know much more than I do about what is recyclable. Moreover, they are able to make useful things from what I considered trash.

Despite their circumstances, Rita is able to maintain basic hygiene. She did not smell at all which was amazing considering she lives on the streets and earns a living from digging through trash. She presented herself with dignity as she shared about her life.

When I said goodbye, I held out my hands to shake with her. At first, she refused and said, "My hands are dirty." I replied, "It's okay, you are doing great work and I want to shake great hands." We all smiled and shook hands as I whispered a silent prayer for them.

I have learned a lot from eating a meal with Rita and her family. I have been challenged to take seriously

Christ's command to "love your neighbor as yourself." I want to become more engaged in the lives of the poor and encourage my church to get more involved.[65]

Reflection and Action

1. Of all the issues discussed in *Visions of Urban Transformation*, which ones are the most pressing in your community?
2. List the three most significant ways you want to apply *Visions of Urban Transformation* in your life.

Acknowledgments

The journey of writing this book was lengthy. I began it years ago while reflecting on the demolition of my old community. The bulk of the writing took place during my sabbatical. I am very grateful to David Palmer and the Servant Partners leadership at that time for giving me the freedom to write.

I am greatly indebted to all those who contributed to this project. Thank you to the staff at Urban Loft Publishers for believing in this book. Thank you to Kendi Howells Douglas for your patience in dealing my emails and delays.

Thank you to Servant Partners staff members who read early drafts while staying with us in Manila for their staff training. Your comments and suggestions helped to shape the final version of this book. Thank you specifically to Wendy Au Yeung and Andrew Wong for your feedback regarding the organization of the book and for fine-tuning the reflection questions. Thank you to Servant Partners interns who helped with some of the general editing and content suggestions. I greatly appreciate your willingness to help with this project.

Thank you to Katie Gard for your very helpful requests for stories and further explanation. Your eye for details has made this book much more reader friendly. Thank you Mario San Pablo Jr. for double-checking verse references for me. Your meticulous work on the tedious job of looking up quotes is much appreciated. Thank you to Matthew, Umesh, Aira, and Mark Timothy for double-checking all of the quotes for me.

Thank you, Lord Jesus, for the hope we have in you to bring about the ultimate restored city in the New Jerusalem. Thank you to my family who allowed me to work countless hours on this project. I could not have completed this book without your love and support.

Notes

1. For an essay (or homily) related to this, see my chapter "Mission: Back to Jesus" in *Passion and Power: Pulpit Messages from the Filipino Heart*, (Mandaluyong, Metro Manila: OMF Lit., 2018), 223-232.
2. Fee, Gordon. and Douglas Stuart. *How to Read the Bible for all its Worth*, Third Edition, (Grand Rapids MI: Zondervan, 2003), 182.
3. Watts, John. *Isaiah 34-66*, Vol. 25, Word Biblical Commentary, (Waco, TX: Word Books, 1987), 156.
4. Gornik, Mark. *To Live in Peace: Biblical Faith and the Changing Inner City*, (Grand Rapids, MI: Wm. B Eerdmans Publishing Co., 2002), 27.
5. Cyrus was acting in self-interest since he wanted the returned exiles to pray for him. God still used this for his glory.
6. Engdahl, Derek. *The Great Chasm: How to Stop our Wealth from Separating us From the Poor and God*, (Pomona, CA: Servant Partners Press, 2015), 240.
7. Perkins, John. *Beyond Charity: The Call to Christian Community Development*. (Grand Rapids MI: Baker Books, 1993), 128.
8. Linthicum, Robert. *City of God City of Satan: A Biblical Theology of the Urban World*, (Grand Rapids, MI: Zondervan, 1991), 172.
9. Benesh, Sean. *Blueprints for a Just City: The Role of the Church in Urban Planning and Shaping the City's Built Environment*, (Portland, OR: Urban Loft Publishers, 2015), 109.
10. Blenkinsopp, Joseph. *Isaiah 1-39*, Vol. 19. A New Translation with Introduction and Commentary, The Anchor Bible, (New York, NY: Doubleday, 2000), 188.
11. More information about the High Line is available at http://www.thehighline.org/.
12. Korten, David. *When Corporations Rule the World*, 2nd edition, (Bloomfield, CT: Kumarian Press, 2001), 2.
13. Benesh, *Blueprints for a Just City*, 136.

[14] Montgomery, Charles. *Happy City: Transforming Our Lives Through Urban Design*, (New York, NY: Farrar, Straus and Giroux, 2013), 132.

[15] Meyers, Carol, and Eric Meyers. *Haggai, Zechariah 1-8,* Vol. 25 B. A New Translation with Introduction and Commentary, The Anchor Bible, (New York, NY: Doubleday, 1987), 416.

[16] Smith, Ralph. *Micah-Malachi*, Vol. 32. Word Biblical Commentary, (Waco, TX: Word Books, 1984), 233.

[17] Bakke, Raymond, and Jon Sharpe. *Street Signs: A New Direction in Urban Ministry*, (Birmingham, AL: New Hope Publishers, 2006), 88.

[18] Linthicum, Robert. *Building a People of Power: Equipping Churches to Transform their Communities*, (Waynesboro, GA: Authentic Media, 2006), 22.

[19] Dawson, John. *Taking our Cities for God*, Revised and Expanded Edition, (Lake Mary, FL: Charisma House, 2001), 101.

[20] Wright, Christopher. *The Message of Ezekiel: A New Heart and a New Spirit*, (Leicester, England: Inter-Varsity Press, 2002), 357.

[21] Do not make the mistake of assuming that this means areas with low population densities are better for the environment. The ecological footprint per person is lower in areas with high population densities.

[22] Watts, *Isaiah 34-66*. 189.

[23] Smith, T. Aaron. *Thriving in the City: A Guide for Sustainable Incarnational Ministry Among the Urban Poor*, (Pomona, CA: Servant Partners Press, 2015), 72.

[24] Jacobs, Jane. *The Death and Life of Great American Cities: The Failure of Town Planning*, (Victoria, Australia: Pelican Books, 1964), 285.

[25] Kern, Paul, B. *Ancient Siege Warfare*, (Bloomington, IN: Indiana University Press, 1999), 4.

[26] Lupton, Robert. *Renewing the City: Reflections on Community Development & Urban Renewal*, (Downers Grove IL: InterVarsity Press, 2005), 35.

[27] Linthicum, *City of God City of Satan*, 168.

[28] See *Slums Reimagined* for a detailed description of the power of self-employment to help the urban poor overcome poverty.

29 There is no internal evidence within Joel that gives an indication when the book was written. All we know is that Joel prophesied during a time of extreme food shortages.
30 Carter, Isabel. *Healthy Eating: A Pillars Guide*, (Teddington, UK: Tearfund, 2003), 8.
31 More information about With Love Market and Café is available at http://www.withlovela.com.
32 Linthicum, *City of God City of Satan*, 167.
33 Montgomery, *Happy City*, 248.
34 See *Slums Reimagined* for a detailed description of how the poor design communities that help them overcome poverty.
35 Brueggemann, Walter. *A Commentary on Jeremiah: Exile and Homecoming*, (Grand Rapids, MI: William B. Eerdmans Publishing, 1998), 313.
36 Linthicum, *City of God City of Satan*, 165.
37 Levermore, Roger, and Aaron Beacom. *Sport and Development: Mapping the Field*. In *Sport and International Development*, Editors Roger Levermore and Aaron Beacom, (New York, NY: Palgrave Macmillian, 2009), 1.
38 See *Thriving in the City* for more insights on living meaningfully and engaging a community for transformation.
39 Ekblad, Bob. *The Beautiful Gate: Enter Jesus' Global Liberation Movement*, (Burlington, WA: The People's Seminary Press, 2017), 41.
40 Bakke, Raymond. *A Biblical Word for an Urban World: Messages From the 1999 World Mission Conference*, (Valley Forge, PA: Board of International Ministries, 2000), 36.
41 Linthicum, *City of God City of Satan*, 247-248.
42 Nouwen, Henri. *Reaching Out: The Three Movements of the Spiritual Life*, (New York, NY: Doubleday, 1975), 156.
43 Bakke, *A Biblical Word for an Urban World*, 5.
44 If the phrase "persons who do not know their right hand from their left" (Jonah 4:11) is interpreted as children, the population was at least one million.
45 Bakke, *A Biblical Word for an Urban World*, 2-3.
46 Perkins, *Beyond Charity*, 30.
47 Perkins, John. *With Justice For All*, (Ventura, CA: Regal Books, 1984), 105.

⁴⁸ Wilkinson, Richard, and Kate Pickett. *The Spirit Level: Why Greater Equality Makes Societies Stronger*, (New York, NY: Bloomsbury Press, 2010), 176.
⁴⁹ Blenkinsopp, *Isaiah 1-39*, 191.
⁵⁰ Bakke, *A Biblical Word For an Urban World*, 35.
⁵¹ Linthicum, *City of God City of Satan*, 197.
⁵² Linthicum, *Networking: Hope for the Urban Church*. In *Planting and Growing Urban Churches: From Dream to Reality*, Editor Harvie Conn, (Grand Rapids, MI: Baker Books, 1999), 165.
⁵³ Linthicum, *City of God City of Satan*, 35.
⁵⁴ Jacobs, *The Death and Life of Great American Cities*, 236.
⁵⁵ Tolstoy, Leo. *What is Art?* Translated by Almyer Maude, (New York, NY: The Bobbs-Merrill Company, 1960), 51-52.
⁵⁶ Servant Partners, *The Nine Signs: What Transformation Looks Like*. 2017, para. 2. (Accessed May 28, 2017. http://www.servantpartners.org/index.php/the-9-signs).
⁵⁷ Perkins, *Beyond Charity*, 102.
⁵⁸ Montgomery, *Happy City*, 160-161.
⁵⁹ Smith, Billy, and Frank Page. *Amos Obadiah Jonah*, Vol. 19 B. The New American Commentary, (Nashville, TN: Broadman and Holman Publishers, 1995), 26.
⁶⁰ Bakke, *A Biblical Word For an Urban World*, 71.
⁶¹ Bakke, *A Theology as Big as the City*, (Downers Grove, IL: InterVarsity Press, 1997), 13.
⁶² See "Called to Remain" by Emma Smith in *Voices Rising* for a fuller account of Emma's story.
⁶³ Bakke, *A Theology as Big as the City*, 101.
⁶⁴ Greenfield, Craig. *Subversive Jesus: An Adventure in Justice, Mercy, and Faithfulness in a Broken World*, (Grand Rapids, MI: Zondervan, 2016), 19.
⁶⁵ Butar-Butar, Ina. Correspondence with author. April 7, 2016.